For Peggy
May you w!
your own
sacred
story
Barb —

THE SACRED SHED
ON THE
EDGE OF THE RAVINE

BY B. R. BODENGRAVEN

B R
Bodengraven

Table of Contents

Preface

Portents of a New Life

I am building a studio, a sacred space—nothing more than a small shed, really. It is taking shape, for the moment anyway, mostly in my mind's eye. It is spare and simple, earth-toned, constructed of wood and stone. It blends in with the back rise as if it has emerged from the soil itself. It has windows that open, a narrow front porch, and rough-hewn wooden shelving. My friend Marilyn's stoneware pots line the shelves. Her round platter brushed with the sketch of an owl hangs in a place of honor. An old mahogany desk, rotting around its joints, that once felt the heft of my mother's hand as she wrote reams of letters to friends far and wide gleams in a triangle of light. Two windows overlook vines and trees plummeting down the back ravine to a vernal pond below. Why am I so intent on building this studio shed? Why now? Why exactly in this spot? Something mysterious is happening. Subtle, barely perceptible shifts are taking place. Shrouded, delicate—tiny tendrils unfold on that shelf of time between waking and sleeping, and ride the waves of my breath. I can't yet say what these subtle messages are. Building this studio, this sanctuary, is a way to find out. It's as if the building of it will reveal the why of it. For now, this is all I have.

As though these barely perceptible movements on the edge of sleep aren't enough to inspire me to begin construction, I also have a dream. Limned in light, my new self makes her entrance: "Can I come in now?" she asks, overjoyed at the prospect of taking over my life. "It's time." I am as delighted to see her as she is to see me, though I can't imagine why. I don't know where my new self intends to take me, or what she means by 'It's time.' Time for what? In my dream, I undergo a complete melding with her, as if melting into mist. "Let's go!" I cry with abandon, all misgivings evaporating in this wonder-filled, pale-yellow light.

The next morning, Frank and I sit in wicker chairs under the back porch ceiling fan, reading the day's news. "We have a visitor," Frank says as he collapses the newspaper onto his lap and listens. Something is lumbering through the underbrush at the edge of the ravine. I see a round-bodied, pelted animal emerge at the rim and stand on its hind legs to observe our grassy clearing. Mink? Beaver?

Hedgehog? I think of all the small woodland and wetland creatures I know. None sounds right. If I had to choose, I would say beaver. I consult my field guide to the nature of New England and discover it's a groundhog. They like to live in moist, marshy areas among leaf litter—which just about says it all for what lies beyond our back porch. I wonder what it is searching for. Perhaps, like me, it is simply in need of a larger horizon against which to measure its world.

But this is, apparently, not it at all. When I tell my friend Jane about the groundhog's visit, she suggests it's my animal totem—a type of "helper spirit." This is a first for me. As far as I know, I've never had an animal totem. She says we all have at least one, often several, to guide us through life. She sends me a copy of the 'groundhog' page from her well-thumbed animal totem dictionary. While living in the Pacific Northwest, she says she was visited by a multitude of animals, all of which brought their special presence to her for some underlying reason. Apparently, the fact that a groundhog has visited me means I am delving into a "deep time of concentration and study." If Jane's reference book is to be believed, the presence of a groundhog also indicates I am undergoing some type of "death without dying." This, plus the fact that the groundhog's presence also means I am experiencing "deep and lucid dreaming," starts me thinking there may be something to this animal totem business. Didn't the recent night-time visit from my middle-aged self suggest it was time for some new version of me to be born?

Bags are another portent of a new life coming my way. The first is a small leather backpack-purse combo that is light and easy to sling across my back as I roam the tidal flats of Crane Beach off-season, pick blueberries at Russell Orchards, or ski across the snow meadows of Appleton Farms. I suffer the same affliction as Queen Elizabeth: I have a deep and abiding relationship with my purse. I can't go anywhere without it, so finding one in the shape of a small backpack at the Kittery Outlets just across the border in Maine is beyond convenient. It's perfect. The others are saddle bags that Frank ordered online for me as a birthday gift. They fit over the rear wheel of my bicycle. I learn that the correct term is panniers. They are French blue (almost navy, only not) with what looks like a sideways *fleur-de-lis* pattern woven into the material, which I also think is perfect. In my new life, I intend to embrace the European bicycle culture. Never mind that Frank and I don't live in Europe; we live on Boston's North Shore. Still, I want to use my bike the way his Dutch relatives do—as an everyday mode of transport. My first destination with the panniers strapped to the rear of my bike is downtown Topsfield. No more excuses for driving the two miles into town when I have library books to return or need to buy a dozen eggs. As I pedal down South Main Street, I hear a lilac bush crying for attention behind the post office. I pull up next to it to breathe in the scent of its blossoms and take a few with me. They are the first things to be tucked into my practical panniers. Their soft purple heads nod over the edge of the bag, satisfied that someone has recognized their glory. I head for New Meadows Market to buy a baguette, but no luck. It's only noon, and already they are sold out. *Tant pis!* Too bad! I had envisioned stowing a loaf, its rounded crust poking out at a slant from my panniers alongside the lilacs. It would have looked so, well, French.

As perfect as these bags are, it's not me who's going anywhere; it's our children—Bethany and Tyler. Overnight, they have become autonomous adults with their own agendas and apartments. After organizing my life around theirs for decades—working part-time or freelance jobs in order to be with them, freeing up afternoon commitments to oversee their homework, monitor activities, and drive them to doctors, dentists, soccer practice, volleyball banquets, and choir rehearsals—I am a mother no longer actively mothering. It surprises me, the loss I feel about this inevitable outcome. I have never felt defined by my children, never had patience with mothers who talked endlessly about their offspring. Still, the natural and normal transformation of our family makes our four-bedroom house feel bereft—or, more accurately, it is I who feels bereft in our four-bedroom house. Either way, within this predictable sequence of events, there is loss as well as gain. The idea for building a sacred-space-cum-writing-studio begins to slide into place. I may not be going anywhere, but I certainly seem to have a new life in the offing. Something is going on back stage. How many lives are we given anyway? How many do we have? One fits right into the other, like a Russian nesting doll, both accommodating and eclipsing everything that has come before.

As if waving my children off into the world were not disorienting enough, I must accompany Mollie on her final foray into the woods. My best friend and spiritual companion for nine years, she came to me in a most ordinary way at a PetsMart canine adoption day, when Frank and the kids had stopped in on a whim. "If you don't come down to PetsMart right now," Frank had intoned into his cellphone, "you will regret it for the rest of your life."

I found my family fawning over an adolescent cinnamon-and-white collie dog with mats under her ears and a long scratch down her freckled nose. She had a beautiful strong square face—not one of those pinched pure-bred collie snouts—and she greeted me as if she had known me all her life. Not all jumpy and yappy, but with a grace and forbearance and gratitude that stunned me to the core, that said she knew something about life. She stood up and latched her light brown eyes onto mine the minute I turned the corner of the dog kibble aisle. I knelt down to gather her in my arms. *"What took you so long?"* she sighed as she laid her head on my shoulder. I was stunned by the immediacy of feeling between us, and, for the first time in my life, intuited a dog's heartsong:

> *For all the love you may not have received,*
> *For all the losses you may have grieved,*
> *I stand before you now,*
> *Never to know any of that.*
> *Still, I greet you with gentleness, dignity, and patience.*

Because I do know that

You are bound by your humanity,

In need of grace and understanding and acceptance.

And—whether you know it or not—

You are in need of me.

"Let's get you out of here," I whispered into her ear.

For nine years, Mollie was my muse. As a one-time, small town reporter, I periodically wrote a column about our adventures together. She became the dog-about-town. "How's Mollie?" people would ask on the rare occasion I went out without her. Mollie, I finally had to admit to myself as well as to others, was getting old. Her best days had come and gone. In fact, she had stopped going on walks with me, stopped climbing stairs to sleep at the foot of my bed, stopped venturing across the kitchen's bare wooden floor unless I made a path of rubberized scatter rugs. It was arthritic bones, urinary infections, fluid retention, and a failing heart.

"Let me know when you're ready," the vet said to me one day when I took Mollie in for a checkup. "There's nothing more I can do."

I would only be ready when Mollie was ready. I trusted her to tell me when. In the meantime, it was difficult to watch her wheeze, hear her moan, witness her slipping backwards down carpeted steps. It was even more difficult to think about losing her.

"Don't you think you're waiting too long?" Frank asked gently.

"She's not ready," I snapped.

"She's not, or you're not?" he pressed.

Mollie entered her last hours as hundreds of tiny white moths inexplicably descended on our front porch at twilight. I lay down with her and watched the winged creatures flutter up and down the storm door. "Have the moths come to spirit you home, Moll?" I asked. She shut her eyes and panted in my face. It was all I needed to hear. Bethany went with me. We sat down on the linoleum floor of the vet's examination room and drew Mollie into our arms, encircling her with love. "We're ready," I said.

And so I began building my shed. The definition and parameters of my former life were rapidly retreating and my new life had yet to emerge. I needed a place apart to begin reimagining myself. A small shed, set back from the house where Frank and I finished raising our children seemed to be the answer, though I am not sure why. As I set about preparing the ground for it, building its rock foundation, insulating, paneling, and staining it, I kept notes of my unfolding life, hoping that this new activity would yield new insights and launch me into a new iteration of being me. Writing in and of itself was not new. I have been keeping notebooks for decades. They started out as just written records of my journey, but then gradually evolved into pages of sketches along with words, watercolor drawings, newspaper articles, and collages. Their main purpose has been to help me process life along the way, especially during my difficult youth. The real reason behind their existence is that I couldn't *not* keep them. There has simply been no choice in the matter. What has become evident in reading through the journals I kept during the construction of my shed was that I was writing out the spirituality I live by. In small word sketches and 'snapshots' of experience, I was writing about life—my life—within its larger context. It was not something intentional, but emerged as a natural outgrowth of my activity. In re-reading my informal pages, it became clear to me that there is so much more to existing on this planet within the parameters of time and space than meets the eye.

The truth is I am amazed to be here at all, living this beautiful, bountiful life on Boston's North Shore. I have been saved more times and in more ways than I can count. Certain episodes of salvation are obvious—once from pneumonia as an infant and countless times while riding in cars without seatbelts as a child in the 1960s, as well as from asthma and a battery of childhood diseases—chicken pox, mumps, and measles—that all kids endured as a matter of course before vaccinations were introduced. Then there was salvation from the sexual predator who nearly succeeded in pulling me into his car when I was 12 years old. And, of course, there's the extraordinary matter of being the last remaining female of my family of origin, seeing years that my two older sisters and my mother never saw. Why I have not followed in their footsteps and prematurely succumbed to a weak heart defies immediate explanation. Interwoven with salvation from physical afflictions, dangers, and diseases there have been resuscitations from grief and depression, not to mention a lengthy, disorienting episode of apostasy. From each, I somehow emerged fundamentally intact if also tattered, or, as my mother would say when assessing an article of hand-me-down clothing for possible continued use, "a little worse for wear."

The shed now sits on the small rise in our back yard overlooking the ravine just as I imagined it would. And my notebooks have morphed into a book—this book. In sifting through my life and the landscape of my surroundings, I have finally recorded what I have always known: That I am, have been, and always will be a human dowsing stick in search of the divine. As to be expected, things have happened along the way. In his classic interview with journalist Bill Moyers recorded in a book called *The Power of Myth*, Joseph Campbell expressed it this way: "You must have…a place where you can simply experience and bring forth what you are, and what you might be…If you have a sacred place and use it, something eventually will happen." Something always does.

Chapter 1
The Green of All Green

I survey the mess of weed and rock and rotting stumps in the right rear corner of our back yard, convinced that this is the designated site. I WANT to bring this studio shed to fruition. I have never been this obsessed about anything before. One idea builds on another, and before I know it, I have an entire three-ring binder of magazine clippings, photos, design ideas, jottings, and sketches relating to building a shed. I am overcome by a singularity of purpose. I research costs of sheds. I make phone calls to carpenters. I see about getting permission from the town, a building permit perhaps. I tend to requirements. On a bright May morning, I find myself at Topsfield Town Hall in search of licensing and permitting officials. I prepare myself to hear that the inspectors I need to speak with are not in, that I will need this form and that form, that my proposed shed construction will require signature upon signature. But, every official I encounter is ready and willing to help, suggesting ways to make things go smoothly, ushering me through the process, helping me connect with people who can make this work. I meet with the conservation administrator, the health commissioner, the building inspector. All are waiting, it seems, to make my life easier. Every door opens on well-oiled hinges. The only issue that needs to be resolved is if I may position my shed to look out over the ravine adjacent to our back yard. Lana, the town's conservation administrator, says she must do a site inspection in order to issue a permit for something to be built that close to the wetlands. We make a date for her visit to my proposed building site, and I head off to the library to peruse magazines and books about back yard building and gardening projects. That's where I come to a greater vision: I'm not just building a studio shed. I'm creating an entire sacred space of creativity and rest, surrounded by benches, a bird bath, a small stone grotto, a shade garden accessed by a flagstone walkway. When I meet my friend Jeanne for drinks that evening, she tells me that the universe is on board with me undertaking this project. Why else would everything at Town Hall have fallen so smoothly into place?

A building permit is no problem, Lana says a few days later, after assessing the distance between the pond and my proposed site. The location is approved! Since the town is applying for increased conservation protection for its vernal ponds, Lana needs to do some research and documentation. She asks permission to access the vernal pond through our back yard and wants to know if I would like to accompany her on her pond explorations. She pulls on her wading boots and water-resistant overalls. I pull on my "Wellies" and follow her into the brambles, descending into the steep pitch of the ravine as we hack away vines and push through paths that aren't there until we make them. Our feet sink into moss as we pass circles of oversized ferns. Once we reach the floor of the ravine, I detect a faint hum. But there is also—strangely enough—a preternatural stillness, as if the ravine's inhabitants are on high alert, observing us from the leaf canopy and hollow logs and are, at the same time, gently quieting themselves to refrain from drawing our attention. Lana teaches me about terrestrial amphibians that live in vernal ponds. She dips her long-handled net into the water and sweeps up tadpoles propelling themselves along with their, as of yet, one set of legs. There are beetle larvae, aquatic spiders, snails, freshwater clams, and dragonflies that cannot fly because they have not yet undergone transformation into "terrestrials." Or is it "aerials?" For the time being, Lana says, they are "aquatics." No wonder I hear a hum. There is an inordinate amount of breeding, incubating, leg growing, wing expanding, and transforming happening in, around, over, and under this water. Lana explains how important the surrounding woodlands are to the inhabitants of the vernal pond. Where would the fingernail clams and fairy shrimp be without leaf detritus falling from surrounding trees? The entire pond would be a non-starter, she tells me. Its food chain would be totally disrupted. As we swat away mosquitoes and inspect the net's catch, I look down to see a sizeable frog with "bulls eye" rings on each side of its eyes staring up at us from a semi-submerged branch. The frog and I lock eyes. I am hypnotized by its bulbous throat bulging in and out as it channels its very frogness to me. I am a willing receptacle for whatever knowledge it cares to impart, though I am too obtuse to catch much of anything.

I am enchanted to think that, along with frogs, both angels and fairies inhabit the ravine's moist woodlands. Early colonists called the hermit thrush "swamp angel." Its speckled breast and light brown back feathers don't readily suggest an ethereal quality, but apparently its song does. The thrush's song is considered by many to be a vocal expression of the mystery of the universe. In our back yard, I have heard birds tapping, cluttering, twittering, scolding, honking, yammering, hooting, and crying. I've heard birds that sound like castanets and one that sounds like a corkscrew twisting open a cork from a wine bottle, but, as far as I know, I've not yet heard the mystery of the universe rising from the wetlands at the bottom of the ravine.

"I don't have $8,000 for this project," I warn Don, who has come to take measurements and submit a bid for building my shed from scratch.

"Not to worry!" he says as he charges up the back clearing to the intended construction site.

"No, really," I say. "I don't want to mislead you. I'm trying to figure out the most economical way—"

"No job is too small. You never know when fixing a neighbor's back door can lead to a complete kitchen re-do." Don whips out his industrial-sized measuring tape and begins to take copious notes.

I hardly think that building an eight-by-ten-foot shed is on par with repairing a door, but I don't say so. Nor are Frank and I thinking about renovating our kitchen. "I just want to be clear—"

"Right. I've got what I need," he says. "I'll get back to you next week." Don's measuring tape zips back into its casing.

Scott, who had come by earlier in the week to give me a bid, was Don's opposite.

"I can be a little needy when it comes to getting projects done," I back-pedaled once I realized that Scott's sense of urgency didn't quite equal mine. "I'm not sure you'll want to take me on…"

Scott ignored my attempts to be tactful as he described various building principles and practices and the importance of striking a harmonious balance with construction materials as well as with the building site itself. At first, I was intrigued by his expansive knowledge, by the thought of materials melding into their environment. But by the time he got around to expounding on tongue and groove vs. post and beam construction, I wondered: Is it *really* this complicated to build a shed? The next week, when Don got back to me, I was dismayed that he had based his prices on a larger sized building than I had specified. ("You won't be happy with anything smaller," he advised.) "I'll throw in a small wood stove to sweeten the deal," he said when he saw me balk at the price. At first I was excited about Don's offer of a wood stove, but I soon saw the folly of having to build and stoke a fire every time I want to use my studio in the winter. I finally called my friend Chuck. "I know this job is far too small for you, but what would you recommend?"

"Check out the pre-fabs," Chuck advised. "If you're working on a tight budget, it's the only way to go."

I envision vinyl, cheap particle board, cookie-cutter floor models. I imagine cutesy miniature window boxes and shutters, not to mention a serious deficit of soul.

On the strength of Chuck's recommendation, Frank and I drive north to visit a pre-fab shed showroom in New Hampshire. Its grounds are full of every small house and outbuilding imaginable—something akin to what I think would resemble a Hollywood back lot. Just as I projected, there are gables and cupolas and shutters and beams and weathervanes and window boxes all affixed to one small pre-fab house or shed after another. Nothing surprises me more than feeling myself fall under the spell of these diminutive dwellings. I am instantly and unexpectedly *enchanted*—not only by their small profiles but by the neat stone pathways and perfectly manicured lawns leading from one to another, as if our yard will look like that if I only agree to buy one of these tiny and tidy structures. I step up into any number of them and envision my bookshelves here, my desk there. I am pleased to notice that I don't see a shred of vinyl or particle board anywhere. Frank and I poke in and out of sheds with names like 'The American Classic,' 'The Historic Colonial,' and 'The Victorian Cottage.'

"I *suppose* I could make this one work," I volunteer, as we inspect a trim little no-nonsense model called 'The Country Carriage.' I like the slope of its roof—almost a "saltbox" style, but not. It has a friendly little porch-like overhang. I like the all-window door option. Light is important, especially in small spaces. If I choose the window-door instead of the solid variety, the cunning oak-leaf-and-acorn door knocker I picked up at an antique shop will have to be mounted on the adjacent wall, rather than to the door itself. I decide I can live with that—this one minor adjustment. The salesman is surprised to learn that I have windows I would like to use in building my shed. (Who actually shops for a pre-fab shed with architectural features waiting in the wings?) He commends my thriftiness and tells me I "absolutely" can substitute the two insulated Andersen windows I rescued from my neighbor's trash for the uninsulated windows that come with 'The Country Carriage.' At the end of the day, I watch him write up my order for an eight-by-ten-foot 'Country Carriage'—a pine, ship-lapped-board shed with insulated flooring, ice and water protection roofing, and shingles the color of mud. It is pre-fab perfection—all for a third of the price of custom-built construction. The cost of the shed includes delivery and on-site assembly. The price I must pay for this cost savings is patience. It takes a full eight weeks for my 'Country Carriage' to take shape on the factory floor.

Jacob's ladder, bleeding hearts, mayapples, goat's beard, lily of the valley. Who knew that shade plants and ground cover read like poetry? Marilyn dug up a slew of shade plants from her woodland garden for me to transplant near what is to be the location of my studio shed. I assemble way too many tools. Somehow, our garage contains a pitch fork. I cannot imagine how it got there, propped in a corner among spider webs and mouse droppings. It looks handy, so I grab that along with a rake, a shovel, a hoe, and a trowel. We have lived in this house for more than a decade, and, up until now, I have kept a sizable distance from yard work. In fact, for the first ten years, I barely acknowledged that we lived on the edge of woods and wetlands. How that ever could have been perplexes me deeply now. The most I can say about this sea change is that one day I opened the front door to let in the morning and was inexplicably transfixed by a blanket of lichen. It was splayed along the trunk of a tree (sycamore, but I wouldn't have been able to identify it as anything but a 'tree' then), as if someone had flung the lichen there under cover of darkness. At the time, I had no idea that there were different types of lichen, or moss either for that matter, and that they have colorful names like star moss, princess pine, and reindeer lichen. On that particular day, on that particular morning, that particular lichen on our front sycamore thrummed. It hummed. It glowed. It vibrated and danced. Its green was the green of all green, or, as the 12th-century mystic Hildegard von Bingen would say, it was the embodiment of *viriditas*—what she called the 'greening power' of life's creator. Its siren song lured me across the porch and down the sweep of the steps. A thought, unbidden and quite unexpected, rushed in hard and stuck: *I am seeing the soul of lichen.* Up until that morning, it was not normal for me to be transfixed by such ordinariness—or what I had, up until that moment, considered ordinary. I had the strange thought that I might be dying. Why else would my senses suddenly be so acute?

Experiences like that are, if not quite routine, more common now that this new version of me appears to be taking over my life. I am astounded by the mottled skin of a tree frog hiding in one of our window boxes, overcome by the intricacies of a scarlet dragonfly's twig-like body, enchanted by mist hovering over the vernal pond as it rises into the treetops. My pulse beats to the calypso of spring peepers and insects—as if their rhythms and mine are one—on late summer evenings, though I cannot imagine the types of body parts one must have to produce those whirring and rubber-band-like noises. I sit on the back porch swing in the dark, in full communion with these small, slimy creatures as they cry out "deep songs" of struggle and exuberance, what Spanish flamenco artists call *cante jondo.* What rough magic has the new older version of me wrought? I think of Merlin teaching Wart, aka the future King Arthur, how to be in empathy with the world. As a child, sitting in a darkened movie theater watching Disney's animated "The Sword in the Stone," I thought it was beyond brilliant that Merlin would turn Wart into a fish so that Wart would understand what it was to experience the world as something other than himself. I, the happy 10-year-old consumer of Disney enchantment, perceived then that experience shapes worldviews, and that understanding other points of view is the beginning of connection and compassion.

Once I start transplanting Marilyn's shade plants, I determine that I really only need the hoe and the trowel. I also discover the first rule of gardening: *Always* place your tools in the same location. Otherwise, as you go between the garage and the garden toting bags of cow manure and retrieving the wheelbarrow for the endless supply of rocks being unearthed, your tools will undergo osmosis with the landscape. A trowel is endowed with an amazing capacity for camouflage, especially when it lies on a rocky slope scattered with leaves and twigs. I talk to the plants as I lay their spidery roots into the moist earth. I pat the ground around their little legs. I tuck them in. Marilyn insists that all the plants she gave me will spread like wildfire. I hope so. When I'm done, the tiniest plot of soil on the back rise is host to a few homesick plants. The mayapples look particularly forlorn. Perhaps they will perk up once they intermingle with the cow manure I mix in among their roots.

On a practical level, building my shed and fantasizing about a shade garden can be interpreted as attempts to get our back yard into shape, transformed into a space where Frank and I actually want to spend time. I site my shed at the edge of the yard, just up the rise from two boulders left behind in the Ice Age. Unearthing the stumps from felled rotten trees is challenging, to say the least. I don't need to get rid of all of them in the vicinity of my shed's foundation site, just the ones impeding my progress to level the area. The problem, of course, isn't only the stumps. It's also the roots—all those invisible tendrils fingering and probing into the dirt below, dangling and entangling their feet into hidden, earthly crevices. I picture them clutching and clinging to their rocky anchors as I dig and chop. I come to understand the expression of "being stumped" more than I care to. I am amazed to find that where there is a stump above ground, there is a cluster of rocks in its roots below. *Rocks have a relationship with roots. Roots have a relationship with rocks.* This is not a thought I have ever entertained before. Any farmer in New England would know this. Colonial farmers complained that they were growing more stone than food, which actually could have been the case. The dynamic of freezing and thawing topsoil pushes a fresh crop of rocks upward, which would have been just high enough to impede the progress of their plows.

From back yard gardening magazines, I discover there is a difference between a rock and a stone—something that astounds me. Through exposure to the elements, freshly quarried rock transforms into stone. It is prevailed upon by external conditions and events, just as we are. In experiencing the crucible of creation, a rock becomes different than it once was. It transforms. It has a story to tell. Only in Death Valley, California, I discover, do rocks actually come 'alive.' During a getaway weekend to Maine, I pick up a copy of *USA Today* outside our hotel room and read about boulders that move across the desert, leaving zig-zag paths in their wake. Apparently, geologists have been studying what's known as "sailing rocks" since the 1940s. Is this some type of hoax? Are invisible aliens at work? The answer, of course, is it is a natural phenomenon. The large rocks begin their journeys during sunny, clear days following rare overnight rains and sub-freezing temperatures. When the wind kicks up and ice starts to crack along the hard muddy and slick ground, the rocks slide along the surface.

Since I am not plowing fields or growing food of any sort except raspberries by the side of the porch, the abundance of rocks in our back yard is good news, though if they could move on their own I would not complain. I collect them to build a retaining wall to surround my shed. Finding just the right heft and weight of stone to place along the perimeter of the building site is a puzzle. I begin to talk to the stones as I place and then replace them where I think there's a better fit. We get along well. While Frank is at work, I dig roots and haul rocks until my back and shoulders ache. When he arrives, he helps me pound in stakes and string a length of twine to form an eight-by-ten frame over the spot I have identified as the building site. It is located under a flowering crab apple tree, whose pale pink buds emerge along its slender branches. The tree's delicacy is overwhelmed by a mess of vines, which are next on my list to tackle.

I find a jack-in-the-pulpit on the forest floor. Actually, I find seven or eight of them, all growing in the area I'm cleaning out beneath the crab apple. If the website I consult is to be believed, this purple and green striped flower develops a fruit cluster of bright red berries in the fall. It certainly looks comical enough. With its tongue-like spadix poking up and out of a fluted base draped by a hood, it looks shy—even coy. I transplant all of the jacks-in-the-pulpit in the area where I planted Marilyn's plants. Jacks-in-the-pulpit love shade. They love forest floors. They thrive in woodlands among leaf detritus and poison ivy. They appear to retreat under their jaunty little hoods. Their very body language shouts DO NOT DISTURB. Where I have transplanted them appears to share attributes with their original home on the forest floor, so it doesn't occur to me until later that in moving them *en masse* I may have disturbed the natural order of things. There may have been a good reason why they congregated at the base of the crab apple. I keep my eye on them and note with dismay that they are not thriving in their new location. I kneel down beside them and apologize. There's nothing to do now but ask them to come back next year.

The area surrounding our back yard clearing is all one great big tangled mass of vines and trees. I am pulling down strangling vine after strangling vine. Some need to be bulldozed. They are as thick as Frank's forearm. Other thinner tendrils have curled and climbed all the way up to the tops of trees, choking the life out of each one, branch by branch. One vine with a massive circumference has somehow made the leap to an overhanging oak branch. I imagine both vine and tree extending tendrils in mid-air, grasping each other under the elbow *a la* trapeze artists in mid-swing. That would have been a dramatic event to witness. I wonder if the crab apple caught that in action. She is no doubt relieved that I am clearing the area of these back yard bullies. She's so delicate and graceful, bowing ever so slightly. My studio shed will fit snugly under her arms, embraced and protected by the "V" of her two diverging trunks.

There is one last stump looming large that I shall have to unearth—along with a variety of more roots and detritus. A concern about deer ticks and Lyme disease flits across my mind as I yank out clumps of weeds and stagger over to my rock pile with yet more offerings. I stand back to admire my work and notice that the crab apple is haloed by a pale-pink, luminous light, as if it's inside the scrim of an oyster shell. A lemon-yellow and black Monarch flutters around the yard, circles my head and flits in and out of branches dotted with tiny pink buds. It lands briefly amid the pachysandra before fluttering out of sight. The robins, too, are curious. They fly in low and hop about the forest floor. Robins are famous for cocking their heads, as if they are listening intently or pondering the universe.

But they are doing neither. Robins cock their heads because their robin eyes are set very far back on their robin heads. They simply want to get a good look at the world—in my mind, an admirable quality.

Somewhere in the far reaches of my mind, I am shocked to realize that I think constructing my studio shed is an indulgence, somehow superfluous. Now that my 'Country Carriage' is on order, my inner critic wants to know how I could be so foolish. She asks why I am giving credence to whims (whims!) that creep in while I'm on the threshold of sleep. With the kids gone, she says, you have three—*count them, three!*—unoccupied bedrooms in the house. Doesn't it make sense to turn one of them into a writing studio? Why waste time, energy, and "good money" to build an ordinary 'old' shed? Then she levels me with reminders of a tattered past: *Is this really a "worthwhile" activity? Don't you have something "better" to do?* The specters of both my parents suddenly loom large. Given that my mother had navigated motherhood under an abbreviated life expectancy, she was big on making the most of every minute of her children's lives, not to mention her own. There was a sense of urgency and intentionality to her actions and advice. Everything had to be "worthwhile," that is, an activity that resulted in either contributing "good money" to the household or improving our characters. My father, having never been encouraged to value play as a boy, could kill an imaginative or artistic impulse in the blink of an eye. "Better" in his mind meant raking and immediately disposing of the leaves in our yard when we kids wanted to rake them into piles and take turns jumping in them. It also meant that, upon arriving home from the grocery store, he insisted on sorting canned goods alphabetically on shelves in our back pantry (peaches always lived next to peanut butter) straight away when I was inclined to stack them into towers and shapes. Having grown up during the Great Depression, self-indulgence and doing something for the fun of it was not part of the lexicon of either of my parents, especially my father's. As much as they instilled in me the sense that life is primarily responsibility and hard work, I have managed to define life as much as possible on my own terms. I much prefer devoting time to artistic pursuits than to chores that can wait until another day. I do things for the fun of it. I do things that I think will bring enjoyment and enrichment. I remind my inner critic of this and repel her contrary nature by insisting that I need someplace else, a place apart, a place given over to reflection, meditation, and interaction with nature. I dismiss her with the words of writer Marjorie Kinnan Rawlings: "I do not understand how anyone can live without some small place of enchantment to turn to." With the wave of a hand, I send my inner critic packing. She will not be allowed to step one foot inside my studio shed. I refuse to be held hostage by her small-mindedness and appalling lack of imagination.

As I order two tons of gravel for my shed's foundation and finish leveling off an area of the back slope, I struggle with what to call this small building that, as of yet, lives only in my mind. Frank observes my activity in researching and prepping for the building of my shed and thinks that it is some logical extension of my graduate studies in theology. He could not fathom why I spent four years "studying God," as he used to say. Now, he's not sure what to make of my penchant for a place of peace and quiet when our home is more peaceful and quieter than it's ever been. I tell him that I intend to use it primarily as a writing studio, but I can tell other plans are afoot. I picture myself carrying a book and pot of tea out to it on gray-fringed winter days. I envision using it as a nature blind, a platform from which to observe the woodchuck, fishers, fox, snapping turtles, cottontails, and white-tailed deer that emerge into our back yard from the scrub of the ravine. I think about using it as my private place of prayer—a chapel of sorts. I tell him that I need a retreat, a common enough impulse for over-stimulated, hyper-sensitive sorts like me, and I tell him that my desire to build myself this retreat just may be what he says—an extension of my formal theological studies. My evolving spirituality is covering new ground, continuously becoming more expansive and embracing of all creation. It recognizes God at work in the everyday details of the world, not in some separate and remote transcendent realm accessed or perceived only through religious institutions and church-sanctioned rituals. At divinity school, I learned a lot about how other people—especially saints and mostly men—defined God within the parameters of their limited humanity. I want to hear more definitively what my own limited experience can tell me. And I want to hear what nature or creation has to say. Mostly, I come to realize, I am envisioning my shed to be a listening platform, where I can ponder and parse the mystery.

Chapter 2
A Sense of Historical Place

Despite the glories of its surroundings, there's not much to our adopted town of Topsfield, Massachusetts. Twenty-eight miles north of Boston on the old Route 1 north/south highway, the town is home to 6,000 citizens—except for a few weeks in October, when the annual Topsfield Fair is in full swing, and visitors as well as Fair personnel swell our ranks. When we first moved to Topsfield, we very much felt our outsider status. Our Kansas license plates, embellished with waving stalks of wheat, were a topic of conversation among our neighbors, who greeted us with what Frank dubbed the "New England salute." A passing wave, and they were off. There were no invitations to coffee or Bundt cakes dropped off on our front porch as there had been when Frank's job took us from Virginia to Kansas four years earlier. Why we found this small-town

New England reserve remarkable, I don't know. We had, actually, both grown up just outside of Boston. We knew the score. But, we had also been away a long time, 20 years to be exact, and had forgotten about New England's quirky state of affairs. At some point after we had settled in to Topsfield, I found myself adopting a sort of arm's length attitude to newcomers myself. A passing wave, and I was off. I recently overheard a conversation between two women discussing a visit to a local church service. One recounted with relief that she had not been approached by parishioners welcoming her with open arms and initiating immediate relationship. "Of course not," said the other woman. "They wouldn't dream of doing such a thing. We're New Englanders."

In Topsfield's historic Gould Barn—restored as a meeting space and intimate concert venue by the town's historical society— I discover that the residents of our adopted town weren't always so indifferent to Kansans. In fact, Topsfield residents were once intimately concerned about the fate of the entire Kansas Territory. During our early days in Topsfield, feeling homesick and upended by our recent move, I walked into the Gould Barn and was immediately overcome. Hanging from its rafters was a political banner that Topsfield abolitionists had created during the 1856 presidential election, when Kansas Territory was being fought over by those who wanted it to be admitted to the Union as a slave-holding state and those who didn't. During that violent and volatile time, Topsfield abolitionists had hoisted the anti-slavery banner high on their shoulders and carried it from nearby Georgetown to

Topsfield in an election-year parade, proclaiming their views for all to see: "Kansas shall be one of this bright constellation. The Union. It must and shall be preserved. Free speech. Free men and Free Territory is our Platform." Like some sort of homing pigeon, I had apparently returned to New England to roost in the only town with clear-cut ties to my beloved Kansas.

It's important to remember that each time and place offers different gifts. I can't expect them to be the same. The difficult bit is in waiting for the gifts to manifest, especially when the realization sets in that it's going to take years to create meaningful new friendships and community. A previous life is never replicated in a new time and place—which, in many instances can be a blessing, as I well know. Though many favorable aspects of a past life may fail to show up in the new, there will always be gifts—one of which could be bright green lichen splayed against the trunk of a tree, or a 150-year-old political banner symbolizing what you have always known: The world is full of underlying, hidden connection.

What Topsfield lacks in instantaneous overtures of friendship, it more than makes up for in aesthetics. Its charms lie in its river bottoms, bicycle trails, rolling hills, colonial architecture, and historic farms. Anyone living in Topsfield is within 20 minutes of the ocean, arrived at along lovely, old meandering roads traversing low-slung stone walls, marshland, pastures, creeping bittersweet, and goldenrod. Then there's Hood Pond, within biking distance from anywhere in town, or the Ipswich River rolling its way through to the sea. It's no wonder that when we first arrived in this pastoral paradise, I dreamed I was an otter slip-sliding along river currents, bellying up and over boulders, skimming along the curl of river banks, and riding the surf in Plum Island Sound. The colonists originally named Topsfield New Meadows, but the Agawam Indians native to this area called this place *Schenewemedy*—understood to mean "the pleasant place by the flowing waters." Hundreds of years later, it still is.

At age 60, my friend Jeanne has left off a high-tech career and immersed herself in the study of colonial American history. She has become enamored with what she calls "a sense of historical place." For several years after we moved here, I wondered about the maker of a carved wooden sign tacked to a tree on Route 1 as the road came up and over the hills from Interstate 95, past two corner gas stations and storage unit business, and into the dense overhang of old maples, rock walls, fields of wildflowers, and wetlands. The sign—black paint against a white background—read: *Committed to Preserving our Rural Character.* It disappeared one day (or night?), and it's been gone now for several years. Its disappearance coincided with the nearby construction of a housing development, whose units are all painted precisely the same buttery yellow hue, on land that was once an untamed expanse for deer and coyotes to roam and ground creatures to inhabit. So, when Jeanne references the North

Shore's sense of historical place beginning to be compromised, and voices her worry about this, I think of the missing sign and the boring yellow housing development. I decide not to point out to her that she and I both live in developments carved from Topsfield's woodlands and fields 45 years earlier. Undoubtedly, we are part of the compromised integrity of the land.

I first perceived Topsfield's distinct sense of historical place during our early days in town, when I encountered the names of Mary Esty, Sarah Wildes, and Elizabeth How carved into a stone marker on Topsfield's town green. After 350 years, the town's historical commission had commemorated the appalling fate of these women on a marker that sits a stone's throw from the town's most significant historic property—the Parson Capen House. Its steep roof and its miniscule leaded windows, circa 1683, identify it as a significant example of medieval colonial architecture. The house, named after its first occupant—Reverend Joseph Capen—no doubt served as an important locus for the community during the Witchcraft Delusion of 1692. Mary, Sarah, and Elizabeth, all accused of witchcraft, would have relied on Reverend Capen for reassurance, counsel, and guidance. I assume, perhaps unfairly, that they also must have received a fair amount of admonishment as well, for— certainly—the young women must have been to blame somehow for these accusations. How had they conducted themselves so care- lessly? What had they done to contribute to this heinous accusation? I imagine the Reverend and Mrs. Capen sharing intense and urgent exchanges about the witchcraft threat spilling over from nearby

Salem to Topsfield Parish. The parson must have had his sleeve plucked, his conscience pricked, his mind troubled by the three women accused of witchcraft on his watch. How had such spiritual calamity infiltrated his flock?

The historic house's dank and musty interior with stiflingly low ceilings explains a lot about the Puritan mindset. It's so dark inside the old dwelling that—even in the middle of a sunny day—I am offered a flashlight in order to make my way through and read the educational cards attached to implements and furniture in the house. A recessed kitchen fireplace that spans an entire wall is hung with wrought iron hooks and handles. I don't need a set of informational cards to tell me that life was an enormous amount of effort then—especially for women. There are candle molds, a spinning wheel, a brass bed warmer, and a variety of other implements and tools that speak to long days of hard labor inside and out. Who knows what else is concealed behind its walls? Puritans hid the bones of small animals inside their dwellings as talismans against dark forces in the universe. They also believed that bad spirits could not abide the presence of iron, which meant that horseshoes were tacked up over doorways and windowsills. Hex marks and daisy wheel designs—potent symbols of good luck and prosperity—were etched into woodwork and at the base of wooden beams. A home needed to be defended both inside and out against "house grims," spirits that meant to do harm and cause mischief to a home's occupants. When I step across the slightly off-kilter threshold of the Capen House and into the bright light of day, I am practically blinded by the sun. I take Mary and Sarah and Elizabeth with me and, in my mind, I set their spirits free.

On a guided tour of neighboring Ipswich following my visit to the Parson Capen House, I am intrigued to learn that "proof" of the devil exists, and that the devil was last seen prowling around these parts in the mid-1600s. The story involves a Puritan minister who delivered a sermon so fiery, so blistering, so unyielding in its condemnation of evil that his words rooted the devil out from where it was hiding among his flock. As the story goes, the devil was so intent on fleeing the wrath of the reverend that it raced up to the top of the Puritan meeting house and hurled itself off the steeple. To this day, it is said that the devil's footprint can be seen preserved in a granite boulder on Ipswich Town Hill, once the site of the Puritan meeting house. At the end of the tour, I go in search of the boulder. Not only do I locate it, but I also identify what looks to be a clawed footprint along its top rim.

As twilight sifts through treetops, I pedal along Brookside Road to Perkins Row, across Route 97 and then across Route 1 to the center of Topsfield. Downtown at this time of day, it's just me, along with a customer or two heading into Cumberland Farms for a gallon of milk. New Meadows Market is closed for the day, as are the two pizza joints, the banks and realtor offices, along with Dawson's

Hardware and the few other modest storefronts along Topsfield's Village Shopping Centre. I pedal along Main Street past the Congregational Church and the town common with its concert gazebo before heading for home along Ipswich Road. The scent of lilacs and honeysuckle wafts around my head and swirls up into the air as dusk descends and, one after another, porch lights flicker on as I ride past, as if my bike and I are some sort of magic wand.

Topsfield is an energetic stone's throw from the old Great Eastern Road of Massachusetts, otherwise known as Route 1A, now lined with gabled Victorians, the Myopia Polo Club, marshlands of plumaged grasses, farm fields, cow pastures, and Wenham Lake. Until I attended a lecture about the historical significance of Route 1A, I had been oblivious to the 300-year-old stone markers at various intervals along the road's gentle slopes and contours. How many times had I zipped by the stone marker at the overgrown edge of Appleton Farms in Ipswich, or—more alarming, since it's in clear view on the sidewalk—the beat up old hump of a stone sitting in front of Wenham Town Hall? That particular marker is chiseled with initials representing the four early settlements of Ipswich, Salem, Wenham, and Boston, along with the number of corresponding miles to these destinations from the stone's location. In recent decades, unsung heroes have been taking weed whacker to underbrush to keep these historic markers clear of debris. Many of the milestones are now supported by two squat stone pillars, casting a gravestone effect across their profiles. I stand before the old pocked milestone in front of Wenham Town Hall and marvel that, in all the years we have now lived in these parts, I never before noticed it sitting there. There are none so blind as those who will not see. In this case, that is me.

It's a bright fall day when I go in search of the Salem Witch Trial Victims Memorial, which is not actually located in current-day Salem. In the 1690s, boundaries between settlements were different than they are today, so it makes certain sense that the memorial is located in nearby Danvers, adjacent to a sports field where legions of small children in neon-yellow soccer shirts gather on Saturday and Sunday mornings. On one particular Saturday, I am the only visitor to the memorial, though there are plenty of people about. They just happen to be involved in a raucous competition for supremacy on a soccer field. As I approach the memorial, my eyes latch onto the names of the three Topsfield women convicted of witchcraft engraved in granite: Elizabeth How, Sarah Wildes, Mary Esty. The memorial's central stone slab is reminiscent of an altar. It is topped with an oversized stone "Book of Life" lying open, with large wrought iron shackles attached to either end of it. (I think "Book of Doom" would be a more appropriate title.) Elizabeth How, Sarah Wildes, Mary Esty—I am connected to them in ways mysterious. They have come to my attention because a new job was accepted, an affordable home in a good school district found, a moving company hired to transport our earthly possessions from Kansas to Massachusetts. The entire sequence of events has led me to a parcel of land where a Puritan community once raised its meeting house in the middle of a virgin forest and condemned innocents to death for fabricated crimes. As I leave the depressing memorial, soccer moms and dads are pulling out of the athletic field's parking lot in minivans and Volvo station wagons. They stare at me curiously, no doubt wondering why anyone would make a pilgrimage to an oversized block of granite at the edge of their soccer field.

Frank and I head to the Gould Barn in downtown Topsfield to attend a lecture about the North Shore's Ice Age. The presenter takes us into the past, way beyond wooden sailing ships, muskets, gunpowder, Agawam Indian settlements, and the Salem witch trials. On this evening, an archeologist has come to teach us about the remains of 45 huts called Bull Brook, an archeological site located just around the corner from a popular eatery called the Clam Box. The Bull Brook settlement predates the restaurant by 14,000 years. Think Paleo-Indians migrating with herds across the tundra, says the presenter. Think wooly mammoths and mastodons. She shows us a fossilized mammoth tooth the size and weight of a brick. I gaze around at the faces of my fellow New Englanders, all so proud of their town's historic legacy—a town common where Revolutionary War soldiers drilled, a unique model of medieval colonial architecture, a plain white Congregational Meeting House topped by a steeple and belfry that boasts a Paul Revere bell cast in 1817 and still tolled by yanking on a thick rope inside its vestibule. Although reminiscent of other times and redolent with meaning, none can hold a hand-dipped taper to the staggering presence of the mammoth molar in our midst.

I should affix a bumper sticker to my car that reads I STOP FOR HISTORICAL MARKERS, though it's not history I am specifically after on my North Shore rambles. I am in search of deeper attachments, a larger context. I want to lift my eyes and cast my vision across a more expansive horizon of space and time. I want to feel in communion with where I now call home.

Chapter 3
So Full of Gladness

As I am about to yank a weed from my newly planted woodland garden, I notice a speck-sized, lime-green insect—the exact color of the surrounding leaf—with legs no more substantial than a hair on my arm. I watch it lift one whispery foreleg at a time to probe the leaf in front of it, as if it were testing the leaf's ability to support its weight. I am astonished to realize that this organism, which has no hope of surviving a summer breeze let alone a New England gale, has room in its speck of a brain for knowledge of the world beyond itself. It is clearly concerned for its survival—and so should I be. Therefore, this leafy foothold for the smallest of organisms remains among the transplanted mayapples and wild ginger. As I purposefully leave the weed in place, it suddenly occurs to me that I am developing a relationship with the land. Our yard is not just a plot of soil supporting a Gambrel Colonial. It is not only a piece of property where I am attempting to plant some semblance of a garden, not just a slice of real estate. Our yard and the adjacent wooded ravine are home to all sorts of creatures and insects that share their habitat with us. As I dig and rake and continue to make the eight-by-ten plot of land ready to receive my shed, I stop to look up. The trees want to know what I am doing in their domain. Maybe it's the patter of a soft rain against the leaf canopy. Or perhaps it's the rustle of squirrels, concealed by vines and weeds, scurrying through dead leaves on the forest floor. Whatever it is, as I work, I sense a presence. I hear something. To quote Ralph Waldo Emerson: "There are muses in the woods." Muses or not, when I stand in my newly cleared plot of earth and look out across the ravine and its pond, I feel the vibrations of the landscape. It pulsates and breathes. I know that Emerson and I are not the only ones to ever register the vibrant energy of the forest. How else to explain the popularity of mass-produced tacky human facial features affixed to tree trunks? I cringe at the irreverence, but I understand the sentiment behind it. Trees are living, breathing souls among us, full of character and deserving of dignity. The poet Mary Oliver counsels us to "walk slowly and bow often," like trees that are so full of gladness.

The wetlands located at the bottom of the ravine adjacent to our back yard mercifully escaped the development that bulldozed its way through this swath of land during Jimmy Carter's presidency. The ravine's natural rhythms have not been interrupted. It is, first and foremost, itself. When I gaze across rings of ferns, statuesque trees iridescent with moss, vines weaving themselves among branches, I am glad that I insisted on double windows for the shed's wall overlooking the ravine. Two windows side-by-side will be all the better for me to view the intricacies of the world where I am, day by day, claiming a place. The muses are moving over to make room for me. The crab apple's arched, slender branches bend forward to ask me in. Day after day, I put finishing touches on the foundation's rock wall, rake leaves, level stones. With all this activity at the edge of their domain, I wouldn't be surprised if the muses were feeling put out. I am, after all, disrupting their patterns—as haphazard as they may appear to be—as I clear a space for my little house. This relatively small intrusion into their world may be able to be accommodated, but I'm not so sure about the other one underway. The same tree company that has promised to grind out a stubborn stump for me on my building site is taking down the massive old white pine along our drive. This should certainly give the muses pause.

"You've got to come down," I say as I lay the palm of my hand on the tree's insect-infested torso. Its trunk has developed multiple weak spots at critical joints and is about to calve right down the middle; it is too dangerous to try to shore up and maintain. This tree that unfolded its tiny head from the berm alongside the lower wetlands a good hundred years ago is dying. The day the arborists ride a crane bucket into the tallest of its treetops, I honor its long life with an apology. There is nothing else to be done. I retreat into the house. I cannot stand to watch its great arms lowered to the ground on chains. As I hear the chainsaw whine into the wood, my own shoulder and hip joints ache in empathy.

I take myself to the Peabody Essex Museum in nearby Salem on a rainy afternoon to see the "Trees as Art" exhibit in the Nature Art Center. The exhibit includes a video created by an artist who tied a brown Flair pen to the end of a branch bending close to the ground, positioned paper under the pen and filmed the branch as it blew in the wind and created a delicate pattern of its movement with pen on paper. Tree art! (Or is it wind art?) Also at the exhibit, I come across the work of a musician who has taken a thin cross section of a tree trunk the size of an old LP vinyl record and assigned a musical note to each of its growth bands, each width of the ring assigned a specific note. The artist transposed those notes to a musical score and played the resulting "song" on a piano. I placed the earphones on my head to hear the tree's life music translated into piano notes and wanted to weep. What else don't I hear in the course of a day? So much of what is sacred is completely unknown, overlooked, or unperceived. In Cremona, Italy—the birthplace of the violinist virtuoso Stradivarius—master craftsmen carve violins from trees felled in only two places on earth: Bosnia and a valley in Italy's Dolomite Mountains. According to the violin makers, these trees rejoice in being transformed from physical substance into soulful, lustrous sound. Every year, in thanks for the trees' wood, the violin makers of Cremona journey with their uniquely crafted instruments to the Dolomites to perform for the forest. I imagine trees clapping their hands in wonder at the adagios rising from the forest floor.

I decide that my studio shed needs to be tethered to our back porch by a flagstone path. I still haven't decided if I will run electricity out to my shed, or not. I can't think how else to heat it, if not with a little portable radiant heater, but I delay making that decision since it is far too hot at the moment to contemplate. In between the plotting and planning, I am drawn deeper into the mystery. It is not just about listening, it's about watching, paying attention. All I have for nature observation is my yard and the adjacent wooded ravine with its vernal pond. As a microcosm for coming to understand the relationships, poetry, and synergy of nature, it appears to be more than enough. I think of the late spring morning four robin chicks hatched in the front mountain laurel. For weeks, I had kept watch on the nest from our dining room window. On the day of days, I sat on the front porch within 10 or 12 feet of the concealed nest—being careful to keep my distance—and realized that I was completely surrounded by robins. Hopping along the drive, swooping in low across the front lawn, perched in branches overhead, it was nothing but robins. They appeared to be *gathering*. Had they received some sort of message? If so, how? It hit me upside the head that hidden forces of communication are afoot in the universe. Clearly, the arrival of these hatchlings has been announced through avian channels. I don't discover until later that this is more than fanciful thinking on my part. Scientists validated intra-species communication decades ago. Bird song decoder Peter Marler recorded bird song with sensitive listening devices developed during World War II. Wave frequency, modulation, and pitch of bird song—all can be detected and recorded in patterned waves on paper. All point to the conclusion that birds convey messages in their vocalizations. In the case of our robin hatchlings, I imagine an urgent all-points-bulletin: *Babies learning to fly! Help protect hatchlings!* The most hilarious interchange I witnessed between robins took place in the side shade garden I am constructing. A female robin perched in the shadows loudly and insistently ordered around a male robin as he darted out into the grass to retrieve grubs. He hopped back to her and transferred food from his beak to hers, whereupon she greedily gobbled down his offerings. There didn't appear to be any give and take, any gratitude or sharing—just a lot of bossing and chattering. It reminded me of how short-tempered I can be when hungry.

Birds are indicators of other animal activities. They flutter and warn and call and announce. And, from my limited observations, they appear to communicate with other species. I also witnessed a chipmunk and a robin make their way across the lawn from two opposite sides of the back clearing. They appeared to be meeting purposefully—both somewhat wary and halting, but coming together all the same. When they met up not two inches apart, they appeared to be exchanging some bit of information as they looked each other in the eye. The robin then flew off into the treetops as the chipmunk turned and scampered back toward the ravine. Interspecies communication—a common series of signals and activity and inflection that conveys all sorts of messaging—is as old as dirt. On a recent Saturday, I awoke before daybreak and lay in silence in the darkness. Then, there it was. At 3:56 a.m., a one-note whistle starting at a low pitch and quickly climbing to another before clipping off. *"Welcome day!"* No translation necessary.

My 90-year-old friend Dorothy comes for tea and tells me that a friend of hers who studies weather and ecology has come to the conclusion that there are no strategies left that can save the earth's environment from destruction. He believes, Dorothy says, that we are doomed. It's too late. Humans have interfered to such a degree in the natural order of things that the earth will no longer be able to sustain life. My immediate reaction is that I don't want to live in a world without birds or frogs. According to Dorothy's friend, there seems to be a good chance I won't. In his worldview, all life on this planet appears to be doomed for extinction. I have my own view of the world, which includes writing about dancing dragonflies, the jerky polka steps of robins hopping forward and backward in the grass, the deep songs of the frogs in the forest. Someone has to love these creatures for lending their poetic and colorful presence to the universe. In the early 20th century, the child mystic Opal Whiteley, highly attuned to the messages of the natural world, was such a one.

She created a sensation with the publication of her fanciful nature diary and later wrote another rooted in the mystical quality of nature called *The Fairyland Around Us*. Like many indigenous cultures and ancient Celtic Christians, Whitely embraced a reverence for all of creation. To her, all was unified and sanctified, redolent with the divine.

Marilyn is a modern-day nature mystic. A barred owl visits her woodland garden and stays for days. The rare trillium grows along her forested garden path. Morning glories, clutching and climbing their way upward with tiny tendrils, attach themselves to her kitchen's wooden-framed screen door as if to say: *"Can we come in?"* At her lakeside cabin in Maine, loons gather at her feet when she sits at the edge of the dock to play Bach on her flute. At her home outside Boston, Marilyn's pottery shed is perched on a partially exposed granite boulder in her back yard. It is her sacred space, her own 'someplace else,' where she fashions clay into pots and listens for the singing to come into their souls.

In constructing my studio and sanctuary, I am giving legitimacy and credence to the pursuit of everyday artistry. Marilyn says people will be intrigued by my commitment to do this, that they will crawl out of the woodwork to help me complete my studio and shade garden, my own natural fairyland. What I really hear her say is this: *I will hold and honor your vision of the world with you.* True to her prediction, many people are intrigued with my intention to create a separate place away. "How do you have time to do this?" they ask incredulously. I make time. Why would I not invest in my vision? My son, the alternative-energy enthusiast, asks if he can help insulate the walls of the shed and investigates the possibility of powering it with solar energy. My daughter wants to lend her decorating skill to its interior and suggests the addition of a woven Native American rug. Frank helps haul stones, construct the shed's retaining wall and, when it's finally built, stain its exterior the color of aging mushrooms. The arborist who rides in on a lethal-looking machine to grind out the enormous stump impeding the construction of my shed asks if he can bring his teenage daughter to see my studio when it's done.

I also have detractors. They react with bemused condescension when I tell them about my plan. They are puzzled by my project, skeptical of its value, and astonished that a full-gown adult would go to such lengths for what they consider to be a childish indulgence. First cousins to my inner critic, they look askance when I explain my motives. "It's going to be my retreat," I say to their dismissive eyes. "A place where I can do art and read and write and pray and be by myself in the woods." Which is not exactly accurate because it's not exactly "in the woods." It's located about 25 yards from the top of our drive, within clear sight of our back deck. But it feels secluded simply because our house is set so far back from the road. I remind myself that being "in retreat" is a state of mind. Total seclusion is not mandatory for creating sanctuary, or for being creative. Perhaps, I allow, a more acceptable response to my detractors would be that I am building my small house of respite and rest to seek solitude from the onslaught of mechanization, industrialization, technologization (is there such a word?), and consumer craziness of the first world. If my unimaginative critics can't get their heads wrapped around the importance of poetry, spiritual renewal, and artistic play, certainly they would understand the need to escape from the frenetic pace, sophomoric television shows, and onslaught of manipulative advertising in the 21st century.

If anything looks like an unlikely denizen of a fairyland, it's a snapping turtle. One the size of a footstool is a first visitor to the area I am constructing into a shade garden. In watching it haul itself up over the lip of the ravine, I think this species may share genetic makeup with dragons. What else would explain the row of diminishing triangles—a saw-tooth ridge—edging the top of its thick, triangular tail? The turtle's shell glows with neon green duckweed. Its feet and legs are dinosaur-like, as wrinkled and old as the earth. Its sharp overbite looks lethal. I watch it rest in the shade of the back rise and give itself what I think is a dirt bath. It then turns around and "fins" its way laboriously back across the clearing and through the brambles before disappearing down the ravine. The entire process lasts about 45 minutes. I am thrilled to be privy to the comings and goings of such creatures, but I am mystified why a turtle would spend so much time and effort tossing dirt around. When I tell Lana about the turtle's visit, she tells me that it was not taking a dirt bath but laying eggs and then burying them. I have much to learn.

I watch a black-winged damselfly that looks like a flying bobby pin whir by the back deck. Its wing arrangement looks more like a helicopter propeller than side wings. Something about its whirring method of moving through the air makes me laugh out loud. I'm sure damselflies and dragonflies are smiling as they whiz about and flutter to a landing on the laundry line. Why wouldn't they? They must be so proud and pleased with themselves. What else starts as a tiny speck of organic matter in a soupy, muddy pond and develops body parts that transform them into aerodynamic marvels?

Certain words resonate. I entertain a few that I never use during the course of regular conversation: Abide, dwell, and realm. Redolent of another time and place beyond the frenzy of the 21st century, they suggest a more peace-filled and serene way to be present in the universe. I am tapping into the core of these words by building a dwelling alongside the realm of a ravine where creatures abide, and so will I. One day, I disturb both a mouse and a toad hovering in the pachysandra. They leap out from their hiding places as the lawn mower engine kicks over. The mouse—adorable. Two black eyes quiver up at me from the grass. Such huge eyes for such a small creature. I think how tragic it is that owls can hear miniscule mouse hearts beating in subterranean mouse nests. It seems such an unfair advantage for a predator to know where a creature is cowering. The toad is all leg, and makes a tall, graceful arc as it leaps into the underbrush. While waiting for my shed to arrive from the factory, I must learn to dwell on the fringes of our back yard forest in the realm of toads and mice.

When I am not dwelling, I am dashing around doing what everyone else on the face of the earth is doing: Chasing down a living, gathering up groceries, distracting myself with possibilities, going to the dentist. In between, I actively work at discerning how to experience and live out my idea of "church" most meaningfully. As an adult I have managed to sift and sort through my faith, separating it from the stultifying—some would even say entombed—structure of the institutional hierarchy itself. Outside its narrowly prescribed protocols and rituals, not to mention its outdated and destructive ideas about women, I have found so much more latitude, so much more dynamism, inherent in my spiritual identity than I ever thought possible.

One evening shortly after moving to Topsfield, Frank and I attended a local showing of a film about John Muir, who, I was intrigued to discover, found his own way into a larger spiritual reality through nature. He did more than dwell in the realm of nature; he succumbed to a kind of religious ecstasy. He fell upon the smallest of plants in joy. He was enraptured by giant redwoods. He perceived the divine everywhere, even in the tiniest insect navigating the vein of a leaf. Despite its inherent harshness, Muir trusted nature's animating and underlying principle of renewal and regeneration. But Muir was no romantic. He knew, as I do, that nature's destructive power is equal to its creative forces. He understood and respected the element of sacrifice—personal loss—inherent in its very dynamic. I have noticed that life's natural dynamics very often call for forgiveness. I think of a meditation I wrote following the tragic death of my son's high school friend:

> *Today, I must open my eyes and start by choosing to forgive an avalanche.*
>
> *I must forgive snow and ice crystals and clouds and*
> *Evaporation and precipitation and freezing temperatures and gravity.*
> *One thing leads to another. I must learn to forgive it all.*

The Jesuit and Indian mystic Anthony De Mello claimed that nature needs no forgiveness because it has no ego. Its elements are its elements. Its forces are its forces. Creation in and of itself is good. There is no intention to injure innocents. A riptide will pull a child as well as a beach ball out to sea. As De Mello wrote in his classic *The Way to Love*: "When nature destroys, it is not from ambition or greed or self-aggrandizement, but in obedience to mysterious laws that seek the good of the whole universe above the survival and well-being of the parts." As one of those "parts" who prays daily for well-being, this is a difficult notion to embrace. Despite its lack of apparent evil or deliberate intention to destroy, nature is not exactly benign. There is indifference. There is injury. There is death. As an earthly creature outfitted with a thin, porous membrane—not to mention a highly calibrated emotional mechanism—that differentiates and separates me from the rest of the world, nature's potentially life-threatening qualities are a lot to accommodate.

I seem to be doing a lot of accommodating lately. Mostly it has to do with the Passat's "Check Engine" light that refuses to turn off. I have lost confidence in the car's ability to take me anywhere without balking and complaining that something is wrong somewhere inside its finely calibrated engine. It's back at the dealer for repairs. But that inconvenience has been trumped by illness—first Frank's and then mine. One minute I am taking care of Frank and the next he is taking care of me. Despite having plans to spend the weekend in Vermont's Northeast Kingdom, we remain housebound. Fortunately, I am not so sick that I can't drag myself off the couch to attend an art exhibit featuring Ipswich son Arthur Wesley Dow at the nearby Ipswich Museum. The museum, housed in an impressive Federalist mansion, contains a small gallery of his paintings: Bright sun-soaked marshes, the Ipswich River in the depth of night illuminated by a full moon hanging in a plum-colored sky, clam shacks painted in primary colors perched along the river's edge. I would have been intrigued to see Dow's art studio, once situated on a remote hill overlooking the Ipswich marshes, but it burned to the ground one Halloween in the 1930s. "Arson," the museum docent explained. "Can you imagine? Why would anyone want to destroy a place where art is made?"

In the oppressive heat we are accommodating, Frank and I stop by the Audubon sanctuary at the end of our street for a swim in the Ipswich River. Only a fresh-water dip will refresh in these cloying temperatures. The itchy sting of ocean water evaporating on skin is an experience we can do without at the moment. As we surrender to the river's current, I am surprised by the water's insistent tug. It takes no effort at all to cooperate with its call. We are not swimming exactly; it's more like drifting. My mind dovetails to my childhood when, at age eight or nine, I learned how to float. I felt then that I had been catapulted into an alternative universe. One minute, my toes had been embedded in lake sludge. The next, my 50-pound body was riding along on the backs of millions of water molecules. "I'm floating!" I had screamed in amazement to my best friend Vicky, whose own two feet were still firmly embedded in the mud. What had happened exactly? I still had arms, still had legs. But someone had flicked a switch that changed my relationship to the world. The entire dynamic had shifted. Instead of a mammal, I was a fish! Maybe I was both!? As I had paddled around Wakefield's Lake Quannapowitt in that newly altered state, I felt a deep and abiding familiarity, as if I had suddenly come upon an old and dear friend in a foreign land. I had, quite unexpectedly, found a new way into the universe. From that day on, I would understand something I hadn't before: Floating changes everything. A half century later, on a stifling evening in August, I lean into a river's current and discover the truth of that all over again.

Another morning of yanking up roots and pulling down vines brings this thought to the fore: *Even when I think I am alone in the yard, I am not.* As I dump yard debris into nearby underbrush, I startle a doe and two spotted fawns following behind her on the floor of the ravine. A slant of sun between the leaf canopy wreathes enormous glowing green ferns, jagged logs and tree trunks saturated with moss, climbing vines, and overgrown brush. I let my bucket of weeds fly. All three deer freeze and lock eyes with me before leaping into the undergrowth. Later in the day, I take a glass of lemonade to the back porch just in time to see all three ambling and nibbling their way along the top of the rise, just above where my studio will be. They don't detect my presence through the porch's large screened doors, and I watch as they daintily pick their way along, ears and white-tipped tails twitching. They make their way toward my shed's twine outline. The fawns are especially curious. What is this new impediment to their land? The doe and one fawn lose interest quickly and disappear into the ravine, but the other fawn stays behind to take a second look. It sniffs at one of the stakes. It nudges the tautly stretched twine, which snaps back, bounces off its nose, and sends the startled fawn diving into the ravine. I am of two minds about deer visitors. The spotted fawns are adorable, especially when they take their rest in a bed of pachysandra at the edge of our back porch. But the abundance of deer here means that they are also a nuisance and can be a danger. They consume the delicate buds of all our purple-flowered hostas and long, orange petals of the daylilies even before the flowers have a chance to fully bloom. They bite my bushes down to the bone, especially during severe winters. They bring deer ticks and Lyme disease. At dusk, they leap in front of cars and cause accidents. Even with all this, these large land mammals lend a sense of wild enchantment to my landscape. Overall, I am glad they are here with me.

How many visits to Marini Farm does it take me to realize why I always pause at the intersection between the barn's doors? Standing at the spot where two oversized double doors perpendicular to each other are open to summer breezes, I feel the smallest of movements, the gentlest of perceptions. The intertwining energy of that location lifts my spirit every time. As I inspected a bin of heirloom tomatoes on my latest visit, the stray hairs at the nape of my neck lifted from gentle air currents circulating across the weathered barn boards. That's when I realized that the farmer who had constructed this barn a century ago sited it at the top of a rise for a reason. He had calculated where to position its two sets of enormous doors for maximum air flow and cooling efficiency. It was as if he had just tapped me on the shoulder and asked me: *Isn't this just the most delicious spot on the face of the earth?* It was the first time I understood that wooden buildings, like wooden ships, are alive with energy.

If New England is sweltering, I make it a point to take a ride up Route 1 to Marini Farm in order to revel in that cross-point of currents. Energized by the scent of sunshine and drying grass, I stand beneath the barn's eaves. I cast my eyes across mounds of blueberries, misshapen heirloom tomatoes, and summer peas encased in what I believe to be nature's most ingenious package: A fist-sized, rubbery "envelope" of sorts in which one pea attached to a tiny green tendril is staggered across from another so that there's room inside the pod for all to grow. I scan my eyes across the airspace above the wooden vegetable bins lining the perimeter of the barn. No matter how hot it is, green, orange, purple, and yellow haloes hover over piles of peppers, potatoes, squash, and eggplants. The barn's entire interior is aglow with color.

At dusk, once the heat has abated, I stand at my kitchen counter with paring knife in hand. It's just me and the fruits and vegetables I bought at Marini's. I make a peach cobbler, a savory tomato sauce, an eggplant parmesan. I work for two solid hours in silence. Frank is away on business. There is no background music, no radio, no computer, no TV. It's only me and the whole-house fan pulling evening air in through wide open windows while hundreds of crickets and tiny singing insects serenade me from outside the back door.

Nature makes an appearance in my doctor's gleaming new waiting room. There are TV screens affixed to two corners, and they are both featuring the same show: A sunny mountain meadow. Cameras pan across mountain peaks, clouds, pine trees, and cottonwoods reflected in a pristine blue lake. There are close-ups of ferns, wildflowers, birds on the wing. Next are undulating waves swirling at the base of cliffs and eddying into caves. It is all so soothing, so pacific. The continuous loop is void of thunderstorms, tsunamis, earthquakes, and wildfires. Clearly, my doctor wants her patients to check thoughts of catastrophic disasters at the door.

I sense the Rockery before I see it. This collection of boulder stacked upon boulder into a circular cave-like structure with tunnels and trails winds up to a precipice that offers views across a pond with a wooden boardwalk and series of small footbridges that remind me of Monet's garden in Giverny, France. Lily pads blanket the pond's surface during the height of summer. It is an enchanted place made by the sweat and strength of Italian stone masons in the early 1900s. That men used muscle and know-how to construct this secluded fairyland is not lost on me. There is no machinery on earth that could design and execute such exquisite intermingling of rock and water. Gina, an artist friend, comes to visit, and I take her to this special place. A bird lover, she creates white-glazed pottery cups etched with chickadees and cardinals and robins. She gives me one of her chickadee cups before I lead her through the Audubon woods to the Rockery, where I know chickadees gather. She and I linger inside the Rockery's stone tunnels, encased in the energy of boulders, as we run our hands along the contour of their massive, humped shoulders. It is a sacred and silent place. We find ourselves whispering, as if we were in church. We emerge onto the boardwalk and circumvent a beaver lodge that has been built up and over the boardwalk at the opposite side of the pond—an inconvenience for human visitors but must provide a comfortable resting platform for lodge inhabitants. We see a mink skittering toward us on the path before it dives into the pond, swims in circles around us, and hops back up on the boardwalk a little farther along. We watch a great egret hunting in the marsh grasses just yards from where we stand. There's also a great blue heron, tiny yellow songbirds, several tufted titmice, and then—with a hint of divine intervention—one of the chickadees chattering just above our heads alights on Gina's outstretched hand.

To see the seashore 1,500 miles inland one must pay careful attention. On a trip to visit my friend Tammy in Kansas, I collect fossilized sea shells along her lengthy gravel drive. They are there—along with marine plant fossils embedded in limestone—just for the taking. I whistle back and forth with bobwhites singing in the wind as I cram small pre-historic shells into my pockets. They are evidence of the shallow inland ocean that once covered these beautiful rolling hills and prairies. As I look up to see a flock of pelicans pass by, I remember that Kansas is on the transcontinental flyway. All sorts of marine birds traverse its skies.

Later in the day, Tammy and I do a little shopping in the nearby town of Wamego, where we chat with a saleswoman who tells me that she is not only acquainted with Topsfield, Massachusetts, but that she has visited several times and done genealogical research in the town library. She reveals that she is related to the Goulds—Topsfield's most prominent founding family. I don't know why any of us are astonished to find connections with people we meet in grocery lines or coffee shops. The truth is we are all bound tighter than we care to imagine, tighter than we ever deem possible.

When I return home the next week, I make another chance encounter. This time it's on the Internet. I discover that Willa Cather—one of my favorite authors of all time—is interred in the Old Burial Ground in Jaffrey, New Hampshire. I am stunned to find that this woman from Nebraska, who evoked the essence of the Midwest so brilliantly in her novels, is buried in New England, within a mere two-hour drive of my doorstep. I take it in my head to make a pilgrimage to her gravesite. Armed with a black wax crayon and sturdy large paper, I kneel down in the shadow of a white-steepled New England meeting house to make a rubbing of her gravestone: *Willa Cather, Dec. 7, 1876 – April 24, 1947.* As I rub the parenthesis of her life, I tell her that I own her entire collection of novels. I feel obliged to explain to her spirit (which I imagine hovering somewhere nearby and listening to my ruminations) that the Midwest is permanently imprinted on my psyche. I feel sure it's part of my cellular memory. It's good to know and celebrate one's unique orientation in the universe. Perhaps it's possible to be a hybrid of sorts, having one foot in the great and glorious Midwest and another resting on the granite of New England. If so, it appears that Willa Cather may have been one of these—as I must be.

On an evening's amble to the Audubon sanctuary, Frank and I meet up with our neighbor Tim, whose house abuts the land. Tim tells us that his next-door neighbor spotted a bear at the edge of the woods. Can it be possible? It's real enough in Tim's mind that he is taking in his bird feeders and trash cans every night. He says that he has heard "things" after dark but that he had assumed it was just deer. Now he's not so sure. I think about the recent bear sighting in the neighboring town of Boxford. All of this is giving me pause. The sun is starting to set, and, in light of this latest piece of information, Frank and I decide to walk into the wooded Audubon land only so far as to what we call the "isthmus"—a small strip of land with marshes and water on either side that leads up into wooded trails. We don't see evidence of bears on our evening walk, but we are riveted by the antics of a river otter frolicking and diving around the base of the arched stone bridge on Perkins Row. The otter, popping its head up to chew enthusiastically while staring us in the face, zips and glides and fishes just below the surface of an entire network of lily pads. It appears to enjoy having an audience. Such a bold little creature! Otters are so unlike beavers, which slap their tails on the water's surface and tell us to "get lost."

Finally! I receive a call from the shed company that tells me the 'Country Carriage' is on its way. My inner critic tries to kick up one final fuss, but I do my own version of tail-slapping. I look out the kitchen window to the stone-edged rectangle on the small rise and tell the site to get ready, that today's the day! That's when I notice that the building site—the exact eight-by-ten rectangle of it—is awash in bright sunlight, which lasts only a moment before drifting clouds snuff it out. The timing and placement of the sun's illumination, its fleeting nature, make me think that the universe is, indeed, on board with me undertaking this project. Something similar had happened several weeks earlier, when as I looked out at dusk, I caught a litter of lightning bugs zig-zagging lazily over the site. How is it that I catch these illuminations? Are they portents? I feel certain there is power in this project.

An enormous flatbed truck beeps its way in reverse up our long gravel drive and stops at the edge of the back yard. The various walls and trusses and beams of my shed strapped to the truck bed must be unloaded and hauled 25 yards up the lawn to the back rise. Three young men, all texting and talking on their cellphones as they lay various shed components out on the lawn, serve as the construction crew.

"We assemble three or four of these sheds a day," says one, when I question him on the wisdom of being distracted by personal devices while hauling wood and holding power tools aloft. "Sometimes, it takes us only 45 minutes to construct this model. At most, it's an hour and a half."

"Piece 'a' cake," another assures me as he tucks a cigarette behind his ear.

It actually takes them a full two hours to construct my 'Country Carriage.' I look at the pre-constructed front wall lying on the lawn awaiting assembly, and I can't get my head wrapped around the position of the door relative to the top beam. I interrupt their comings and goings and cellphone usage.

"There's a problem, guys." I pause for dramatic effect. "The door's installed upside down."

The young man who deigns to answer doesn't glance at the door. "We always put doors on this way," he says.

"If you do," I say, "you're making your customers step up and over an enormous threshold to get inside their sheds."

An Amish barn-raising it is not. Bethany, who has taken the day off from work to witness my shed's construction with me, can tell I want to box their ears. How can they be so cavalier about assembling my sanctuary? I see the crew inspecting the door and conferring. They have agreed with my analysis of the problem and are now dismantling the door from its frame and making adjustments. When the insulated floor has been put into place, the walls are up and the roof trusses fitted and shingles on, I do a final inspection of their work. I open the white-framed window-door that has been righted and step up into my studio. Just as I imagined, the salvaged Andersen windows side-by-side on one wall provide an open vista onto the ravine. The brand new awning, or crank, window I saved from my neighbor's trash along with the Andersens is centered in the opposite wall. The back wall is windowless; it's waiting for shelving and an array of nature treasures and books. I am enraptured by the scent of fresh wood, the feel of the floor beneath my feet, the rise of the open-beamed ceiling. I also note a few nails positioned improperly in the studs. I see the dirty imprint of the crews' waffled boot prints on the floor and some even on the ceiling trusses. I note the areas of the exterior where wood filler was not sanded properly at the factory. I tell the crew that I am amazed by their efficiency and thank them for repositioning my door but that my 'Country Carriage' is not going to be a tool shed where finish might not matter. I need the few imperfections addressed. Since the day is almost done and they have yet another shed to assemble in 45 minutes or less, they suggest I call the office and ask the manager to address my concerns. I agree that this will probably be best and wave them off down the drive. Bethany and I gather a broom and window cleaner and get to work tidying up the interior. I tell my 'Country Carriage' that from this day forward she is no longer just a pre-fab shed. I tell her how pleased I am to finally have her here with me and that everything will be brought to order all in good time.

Bethany and I sweep the floor and scrub the windows and wipe footprints from wood, all the while laughing about the protestations of the construction crew, something we find hilarious now that they are gone. *We always put doors on this way!* I laugh and shake my head and call the shed company receptionist who tells me that a manager will be out next week to clean up remaining details. The company wants me to be a satisfied customer. Satisfied? I'm elated! As we finish up for the day, we turn to admire my new little woodland house under Miss Crab Apple's sway. Bethany says the stone wall encircling the shed reminds her of a bird's nest. The idea sticks in my mind. I am not at all surprised to find that in his book, *The Granite Kiss*, master wall builder Kevin Gardner describes stone walls as "the result of…elements already present in a landscape. They are, in a way, equivalent to a bird's nest…" If I was searching for a name for my little house, I need look no further.

It comes as no surprise that birds are the first to investigate. They swoop in low and hop and fly about, landing very near as I sit perched on the shed's threshold. Despite the newly christened name of my studio, I can't tell one type of bird from another—beyond robins and cardinals, that is. I make a mental note to keep my bird identifier in the shed. There is so much activity on the edge of the ravine, so much to distract me, that I wonder how I'm ever going to get anything done. For now, in its nascent state, I gaze out its windows, revel in its simplicity and observe the coming and going of chipmunks and birds. For the time being, the deer are staying away, no doubt spooked by the crew's lingering cigarette smoke and power tool racket.

The next week, the manager from the shed company arrives to take care of the finishing details. When he's finished, he hands me two keys to the door—something the construction crew overlooked during their hurried exit. Next task on my list is to build stairs and a small landing along the front wall. I must also insulate and panel the interior and construct wall-to-wall shelving. The most important task before winter sets in, though, is to get a coat of stain on the unfinished exterior.

The entire world is turning a muted bittersweet orange, which can only mean one thing: It's fall, and the Topsfield Fair is in full swing. Every year I go to the giant pumpkin weigh-off—a great big hullabaloo over hideously obese, lopsided gourds that are lifted and weighed with the help of a forklift. They are so immense that no man could actually put palm to pumpkin and hope to hoist it a centimeter. It would take Paul Bunyon armed with a chain saw to carve them into jack-o-lanterns.

"Whaddya think, folks? Let's give it up for this beautiful 1,391-pound beauty!" cries the emcee over the sound system in the Fairgrounds' big old drafty arena blown through with the smell of animal hide, hay, and manure. Those of us crammed into its bleachers clap heartily for the unsightly mottled gourd. It, like all the other milk-fed pumpkins competing for recognition, is lolling sideways on the arena's dirt floor. There's something slightly obscene, or grotesque, about its size. Its impressive weight is broadcast on the wall-mounted neon score reader. A few minutes later, another misshapen orange mass is hung from the scale. The barker yells excitedly into the mike that it weighs 1,513 pounds! Impossible! Amazing! The crowd is astonished, but I'm not sure why. The previous year, the world record was set by an 1,800-pounder. Finally, after several hours of weighing obese entrants, it is determined that the winner of the Topsfield Fair Pumpkin Weigh-Off is a 1,668-pound bruiser. It is hung with ribbons and put on display in the Fairgrounds' fruits and vegetables building.

During our first years in Topsfield, when I worked as a part-time reporter for the local newspaper, I was assigned to cover the giant pumpkin weigh-off. I didn't realize what a plum assignment it was. When I arrived at the arena, I, along with hordes of photographers and other reporters swarmed the behemoths. One Japanese media outlet had sent a delegation of broadcast reporters to cover the event. Their sophisticated video equipment hemmed out the rest of us. I imagined millions of Japanese peering curiously at their television sets and computer screens while trying to divine the American mindset from pixels of giant pumpkins.

Every October, the Topsfield Fairgrounds are abuzz with massive trailers, RVs, pickup trucks, John Deere farm equipment, carnival tents, a carousel, tilt-a-whirl and a Ferris wheel. The entire town smells like a cross between a fried dough factory and a pig sty. The parade used to be the kickoff to the entire week-long event, but somehow, instead of serving as the catalyst of excitement, it now plays second fiddle. After the pumpkin weigh-off, the runner-up pumpkin is fork-lifted onto the bed of an antique pickup truck and leads off the parade. The entire extravaganza takes all of 25 minutes from Topsfield common to the Fairgrounds, which is just enough time for a few local politicians, a perky Mrs. Essex County, high school marching bands, Clydesdale horses pulling antique fire engines, and a cavalcade of scout groups to march by. Then follow ten days of traffic jams up and down Route 1 until the Fair is over for another year.

There is something about large, live poultry that has me spooked. Behind wire mesh at the Fair's poultry house or contained inside fencing along Topsfield's farmlands, they don't feel so menacing. But when wild turkeys get a little too close at the Sisters of Notre Dame de Namur acreage in nearby Ipswich, I get skittish. Wild turkeys can be nasty creatures. When I look out my office window and watch groups of them run—necks fully extended forward, wings slightly arched along their back—across the swells of the Sisters' fields, they look like a herd of miniature dinosaurs. There is something hostile and blank and stupid about their demeanor. I go out of my way to avoid them when I come and go from the office.

The Sisters, who travel to the most desolated and devastated areas of the earth for their ministries, must surely scoff at my hesitation to confront a few wild turkeys on my way out to lunch.

Because my job with the Sisters is located on the outer edges of Ipswich, it doesn't take long for me to get to Crane Beach after work. I keep sandals and Capri pants in the car so I can make a quick change and get out to the sand flats to watch the tide run out and the sun dip into the evening sky. The fall, especially September, is an exquisite time to go to the barrier beaches, and wander out along the rippled sand paths. I leap over mini rivulets rushing out to the surf, or walk barefoot inside their watery paths. I find lone feathers from piping plovers and gulls. I kick at broken shells and driftwood along the tide line. I create temporary beach sculptures of barnacle-crusted crab shells, driftwood, and other items washed up by the tide. One late afternoon, I walk way out to an abandoned gnarled tree trunk, dried and twisted, sticking up along the dunes. Next to it is an abandoned beach chair open to its sitting position, lodged ankle-deep in sand. The chair is both dry and welcoming. It appears to be waiting for me. I sit down and pat the adjacent upended tree while listening to the far off "shush" of the retreating ocean. At that moment, everything feels soft: The breeze, the chair, the sand, the clouds, the late afternoon light, the collar of my cotton blouse rippling against my neck in the breeze, the "shush" of the surf. It is out among the ridges of sand, sitting in the abandoned beach chair that will be overcome by the tide in another four hours that I process that I am suddenly, immensely, and gratefully glad to be alive.

Fox hunts, dog sled races, scavenger hunts—depending on the time of year, I never know what I'll encounter on the trails of Appleton Farms. One of North Shore's most historic public properties and the oldest working farm in this country, Appleton Farms' wooded trails and farm fields are a tonic. It's Columbus Day weekend in mid-October, and Bethany has come up from the city for a visit. We decide to go walking on the Farms' wooded trails. It's overcast, brisk and breezy, and we are in for a good long walk when we encounter what appears to be the entire contingent of North Shore's landed gentry. They are dressed to the nines in cardinal-colored hunting jackets with flashing gold buttons, polished knee-high black leather boots, and rounded double-brimmed black velvet hats as they sit nobly astride their steeds. It's the annual fox hunt of nearby Hamilton's Myopia Hunt Club. The magnificent black and mahogany horses are prancing and pawing the ground, reined in by a swarm of barking bloodhounds. The dogs stride up to Bethany and me along with a clutch of other gaping onlookers as if to ask: *How dare you interfere with our hunt?* Actually, there's no question about it. Beagles and hunting hounds with a collective air of self-importance bark at the horses to quit being so impatient to get going. They bark at us onlookers to tell us to get out of the way. I am uneasy, clearly not in my element, and hoping that there is no live fox being hunted. Surely, the club has rigged up some fabricated substitute as quarry?

A recent perusal of several health magazines while waiting in the grocery check-out line confirms what I've always known: "Forest bathing" is medicinal. In fact, judging from the number of articles I come across within a five-minute wait time, it seems to be all the rage. The 'Need to Know Health Tip' of one of the magazines touts the benefits of fresh, moist, earthy air for overall health and well-being. The author claims that the Japanese are addicted to *shinrin-yoku*—otherwise known as "forest bathing." As far as I can see, this seems like a benign, if not beneficial, addiction. According to the article, the benefits of forest bathing are substantiated by scientists. They have discovered that it not only reduces stress and blood pressure, it also increases cancer-fighting cells. When it comes to aromatherapy, the earthy, peaty smell of rotting plants and trees is apparently better than any lavender- or lilac-scented candles. Bethany and I lay the palms of our hands on the trunk of an old oak tree and feel its respirations and circulations. We breathe in the exhalations of its leaves as we strew buttercups and joe-pye weed around its base. We have bathed in the forest and we are cleansed.

Chapter 4

Boundaries are Porous

There are pockets of coziness in the universe, and on a Friday morning the week before Halloween I stumble upon one. I am adrift in reverie before a wood fire inside the Russell Orchards barn that, no matter the season, is permeated with the musky scent of ripening apples and wood smoke. Like the abandoned beach chair on Crane Beach, the lone wooden rocker in front of the fireplace is unoccupied and seems to be waiting for me. I slide into its worn contours and rock its bent frame over the hard grain of the floor. It is wood on wood, while more wood combusts into flame inside the old stone fireplace. I only intended to run in to buy a few Macs for an apple pie. Yet, here I sit, surrounded by bottles of blueberry and blackberry wine, jars of local honey, and the scent of 'old-fashioned' plain doughnuts baking in the barn's adjacent kitchen. I fall into what I call a "fire trance." Why would I ever want to leave?

I often go out exploring, and—when Frank is busy and friends are scarce—very often I go alone. I don't let traveling solo stop me. Being comfortable and content to go places alone is one of the great gifts of age. So, when the opportunity comes one cold, dark evening to attend a chamber concert for a mere $15 at the enormous cliff-side Crane Estate, I go. Everyone I ask to accompany me is busy, so I go alone. Why would I pass up the chance to ride sound waves of Telemann's "Trumpet Concerto in D" inside a grand ballroom of cut-glass chandeliers and parquet floor while the echo of churning surf drifts through French doors closed tightly against the evening's chill?

The next weekend, Maine beckons us. On the way north, Frank and I stop at Plum Island to stretch our legs before the three-hour car ride up to the north country. The air is unsettled, windy, gray. The marsh grasses that crowd tightly along the edge of Plum Island's nature boardwalk are 10 to 12 feet tall. Their top plumage waves wildly in the blow. They bow and bend in unison, as if they are paying homage to us as we walk by. On up we drive to Owls Head Light State Park on Penobscot Bay, where we position beach chairs in a prime location to watch the sun set. The gift of our three-day get-away? Eating chocolate-covered blueberries and sipping chilled Riesling from a local vineyard as surrounding cliffs turn to burnished copper and a restless sea pulsates in the dying day. It does not escape me that some of life's supreme moments happen while sitting in two low-slung old beach chairs on the edge of evening.

I know there's a scientific explanation for mist, but I prefer to dwell in its mystery. I love its mystical mantle, its veiling of treetops and trunks, its other-worldly illumination by an isolated slant of sun slicing into the Ipswich River. Every morning, I drive to work along the Ipswich River from Topsfield to Ipswich—first along the stretch called Ipswich Road in Topsfield and then along Topsfield Road in Ipswich. There is sense in this. Nineteenth-century travelers in Topsfield heading for Ipswich would have named the road for their destination, and vice versa. On the morning of the mists, I pass the three "chocolate" horses that graze together every day in a pasture along this dual-named road. I have named them according to the color of their coats—Dark, Milk, and White. Sometimes the horses are buckled into rain capes of forest green, eggplant, or a red tartan. It makes me laugh to see them dressed in such finery, as if they are stepping out for an evening's entertainment.

The gray day provides a startling backdrop for the incandescent colors of fall—the burgundy-tinged marsh grasses along the river, the maple and birch trees with leaves glowing salmon, saffron, butternut-yellow, and olive-green. All are fireworks in a muted framework. Brilliant, bright-red winterberries glow among the underbrush of the ravine while everything else in nature is busy hunkering down and pulling a blanket up to its chin. On the banks of the ravine's vernal pond, turtles are entering hibernation. Wood frogs are turning into amphibious ice cubes, their perfect little suction-cupped foot pads and resilient legs sliding tightly in place alongside their tiny torsos. They resemble small stones on the frozen forest floor. Who can tell them apart? When it comes to frogs, it seems as though cryopreservation—bowing out from life temporarily with the help of freezing temperatures—is part of the plan. Their spring awakening is either resuscitation or full-blown resurrection. Maybe both. Either way, the frogs that keep me company throughout the spring and summer freeze at the first touch of Jack Frost and don't actively enter the land of the living again until four to six months later. Within a few hours of prolonged, moderate temperatures they are completely thawed, reoriented to the world, and begin mating with abandon.

In the middle of the night, I awaken to hear owls duetting loudly outside our window. I get out of bed and creep over to the windowsill to peer into the darkness. I think on the time Mollie had roused me from sleep shortly after we adopted her. She nudged open the door of the master bedroom, upended my blankets, and pushed at my shoulder with her nose until I got up to go with her to the open window. She and I crouched silently together in the dark, "who-whoooooooos…" echoing in the night air. We had hung suspended in that moment, surrounded by the dark, enthralled by the duetting owls, as we eavesdropped on another world. "They're telling each other stories, aren't they, Moll?" I had whispered into her ear. She nudged my cheek as if to say, *I knew you would understand.* In that moment, despite the fact that we weren't of the same species, Mollie and I were of one mind, equally enchanted with the world, "spirit sisters," or "soul friends," for life.

I discover that a naturalist with expertise in owl behavior is coming to a local library, and I make it a point to attend. Marcia has several types of owls with her. One by one, she invites them to step out of their wooden travel crates and onto her gloved forearm to meet the audience. We either coo or gasp, depending on the size and majesty of the bird that emerges. They are magnificent, intelligent creatures. Their eyes pierce us with knowing and intensity. None are as riveting as the barn owl—with its funny little heart-shaped face— that had hatched in captivity and immediately imprinted on humans. When Marcia presents it to the packed meeting room, it looks all of us over carefully and with much interest. It seems to be taking a reading of our faces. The barn owl may have a human imprint, but, in watching Marcia interact with her charges, I am convinced she has an 'owl imprint.' She tells us that she grew up around owls and learned their varying hoots and calls as a six-year-old. Her beautiful and thick, long gray-blonde hair is clipped back with an owl-feather barrette so that her hair gives the impression of plumage. I am mesmerized by her interaction with the owls and enchanted with the birds. I don't know who is most fascinating to watch—the owls or Marcia.

Overnight, an unsettled wind blows through, ushering in an unseen yet palpable presence. I hear the rush of leaves twisting and twirling as they cascade down the ravine while branches break from limbs and thud to the ground. They creak and groan, like a Greek chorus, in the nether reaches of my sleep. In the morning, the sky is dashed to a dark gray. Suddenly, the lights flicker and dim as I set the table for breakfast. It's unsettled and uneasy. Something's coming. A cacophony of starlings confirms this as I go out for my morning walk to the old stone bridge on Perkins Row. And then, again at noon, the starlings are screeching and twittering and darting around in trees all around our house. There is so much edgy energy in the air that I can hardly concentrate on the tasks at hand. It's a long, slow build-up to a wild rainstorm that arrives the next night. Just as Mollie's unusually agitated behavior used to warn me of an approaching tornado when we lived in Kansas, the birds and creatures of the ravine put out all-points-bulletins about coming storms.

In the gray of a late November day, I take a ride up to Newburyport to see the city's storefronts strung with pine garlands and white lights. Thick fog in the harbor sails slowly, silently, up the brick buildings and cobblestones of State Street. Soon, the entire downtown feels as though it is enmeshed in bubble wrap. Decorative lights framing display windows are barely visible, their tiny, white bulbs hardly making a glint or dent through the fog. I feel as though I have blinders on, that I need radar to navigate this disorienting haze. On the way home, the fog dissipates as I drive inland and head down Route 1. Suddenly, the sun breaks through and is setting behind pale-yellow and pink feather clouds, disappearing behind ridges of black pine. I pull over to watch the show. On either side of the two-lane highway in Newbury, the Great Marsh sweeps the horizon. I am staggered by the sun's sudden brilliance after being confined by the fog. I am mesmerized by the predictable. Haven't I seen thousands of sunsets glinting off the surface of hundreds of rivers? Doesn't the sun set every day? Not like this, I tell myself. It doesn't always rim the underside of clouds with pink the color of crab apple blossoms. I am on a concrete island roadway bisecting this magnificent natural water filtration system that extends 20,000 acres up the New England coast from Cape Ann to New Hampshire. The Parker River flows through its midsection, carrying and filtering sediment up and down the land. The sunset is over too soon, and I continue on my way home, stopping at Mill River Winery—a recently renovated old cider mill along the side of Route 1—to buy a bottle of their home-blended Plum Island red. Frank and I toast the dying of the day at the kitchen island around a spread of Wensleydale cheeses and crackers.

Forest creep can happen to any house, even to a magnificent Arts-and-Crafts specimen constructed of fieldstone that looks solid enough to withstand a cyclone. Even stones are prey to vine tendrils and tentacles pushing into cracks and crevices. It happened to the Willowdale Estate in Topsfield's Bradley Palmer State Park. Vines crept along its foundation, crawled up its walls and strangled its chimneys. For decades, it could not breathe. It was a shell of a ruin. Shortly after moving to Topsfield, we discovered Willowdale by accident as we explored Bradley Palmer's walking trails. "What a shame," I sighed as I backed away from rotting French doors adjacent to an expansive patio. We picked our way around chunks of thick yellow icicles that had fallen from the eaves. The French doors were filthy, covered in years of grime. *No Trespassing* and *Keep Out* signs were tacked up across shutters hanging askew from rusty hinges. As we peered inside filthy windows, we saw a grand wooden staircase woven with enormous cob webs, inlaid wooden floors covered in dust and debris. The home's bones, once so elegant, were dilapidated, sagging and despondent. Abandoned. Mice and other forest creatures must have been having a field day inside cupboards and closets. It was hard to imagine ladies in tea dresses and broad-brimmed hats alighting at its doorstep. There had been garden gatherings, hunting parties, equestrian events, balls, and cotillions. This was, we were to learn, the country estate of Boston lawyer and industrialist Bradley Palmer, who built the house on the banks of the Ipswich River in 1901 as his summer retreat. Little did I know when we first discovered the abandoned mansion that arrangements were then being made for its expansive restoration. A hundred-plus years after its construction and six years after we moved to Topsfield, Willowdale was transformed into a stunning backdrop for weddings, private parties, and other special events.

On a winter's evening, as Frank and I approach its now grand entrance, tiny white lights twinkle on boxwoods and lamp posts. An enormous swath of evergreens tied with a sumptuous red bow hangs on the mansion's cranberry-colored front door. Since its renovation, the mansion is routinely thrown open to the public. Guests are invited to wander through its exquisite interior, including up the restored staircase that leads to private rooms where brides and grooms compose themselves before nuptials. As I wander from room to room, I decide that conversation must have been a form of valued entertainment in the beginning of the 1900s. The mansion has so many inglenooks—cozy wooden corner benches—built into walls and along the edge of its multiple fireplaces that party-goers and visitors had no excuse not to engage in intimate chats. There's even an inglenook around the small-scale fireplace inside the elaborate master bath on the second floor. I can't imagine who would have been invited in to chat while the master of the house was taking his *toilette*.

On the night Frank and I visit the mansion, a Christmas tree holds sway over the library. Reception tables are spread with red-velvet cupcakes and homemade gingersnaps. The scent of chocolate wafts across the dining room, where we are greeted by our gracious hosts. I am intrigued to note that, a hundred years ago, even such utilitarian objects as doorknobs were works of art. Whether carved metal or cut glass, all of Willowdale's restored doorknobs glitter like jewels, along with every floorboard, Delft tile, and pane of stained-glass. We assemble in the ballroom to watch three opera singers in evening gowns assume their position before the carved-marble fireplace. I gaze up at the two-story, half-timbered ceiling, take in the decorated wall sconces, and string of lights snaking among greenery along the exquisite mantle. Just as the trio lets loose with "Joy to the World!", I notice that the singers' profiles are framed by carved marble angels.

Some streets, like people, serve as connectors. Asbury Street, where Bradley Palmer State Park fronts the civilized world, is one. It connects the flat lands and open fields of Hamilton to Topsfield's more dense woodlands and wetlands. Turning into Asbury Street from Hamilton is to climb gently along curves and turns before reaching what I call the "Trinity Tree," in competition to be the most majestic of all Asbury's towering trees. Three solid trunks fan out from the base of one stump, where it sits at a dangerous bend in the road. Next it's on to the homestead of World War II General George Patton—a friendly, white-framed farmhouse—and modern-day gentlemen farmer's mansions and barns. At the peak of a hill overlooking the Audubon sanctuary on one side and Bradley Palmer State Park woodlands on the other is the enormous copper beech, with massive humped roots that resemble elephant feet and branches that swoop down to the ground and curve gracefully back up toward the sky. Its presence adds an unstudied grandeur to the square gray mansion located in its shadow. When driving along Asbury Street in summer, so much overhead foliage crowds out any waning sunlight that it feels like 9 p.m. when it's an hour earlier. The trees' dense undergrowth creates camouflage for roaming herds of white-tail deer, whose eyes—small glowing balls eerily suspended in the darkness—peer over stone walls before leaping off into the forest or dashing across the street. Finally, the narrow road winds down to the river bottoms of Topsfield near the entrance to Bradley Palmer. The Ipswich River announces its presence with a pungent, wet smell of mud and plant decay wafting in through the car windows. If I shut my eyes at just this turn of the road, I would know exactly where I was without seeing a thing.

🍃 🍃 🍃

Inside the stately, white-steepled Unitarian Universalist Meeting House in Newburyport a few weeks before Christmas, the lights are dim. I am wearing my shawl-collared sweater the color of muted pumpkin. Candle flames are flickering up and down the enormous clear-glass windows that line the austere meeting hall. Its simplicity is beautiful, but also hypnotizing. I find myself beginning to nod off and head out somewhere ethereal at the outset of the concert. Despite the blaring of the brass, the crescendo of the choir, the hard and narrow box pew of a meeting house built 200 years ago, I am descending into a dream state. All the music is about mystery, majesty, the Messiah. As at the recent Willowdale Christmas concert, there is a sense of the majestic among us. I am surrounded by wonder. Why can't I stay alert? A story so amazing that it can hardly be believed is being proclaimed, and I'm nodding off inside my shawl-collared sweater.

I am drowning in food preparation: Christmas sweet bread, cheese and spinach balls, scalloped potatoes, hot apple cider, chicken skewers with peanut sauce, spiral ham, Black Forest cheesecake. So many arrangements. So much gift organization. So much of making things festive and fun. And this is for only a dozen people. I can't imagine hosting a holiday party for 25 or more. I would be done in. This Christmas turns out to be a brilliantly sunny and ice cold day, as my poet daughter says, a "silver" day—one in which we drive the 40 minutes to Rockport so I can ring hand-bells out over the waves from atop the town's granite cliffs. "Merry Christmas!" I call into a cold wind as I alternately ring one bell and then the other. "You're a little loopy, Mom," Tyler says, as he jams his hands in his pockets and hunches down into the collar of his coat. He refuses to participate in such unrestrained joyous shenanigans, though he need not feel embarrassed. The one or two groups of other visitors huddled along the granite outcropping don't give us a passing glance.

Bells are harbingers of news, which today involves a certain something happening in a manger long ago in Bethlehem. The news doesn't have much of a chance of being heard. The wind throws a blanket over the bells even before their sound can reach the surf. On our return to Topsfield, I ring the bells out over the ravine to wish all its buried, hibernating, frozen, and migrating inhabitants a merry Christmas day. The evening descends in a dusky pale-blue and yellow wash as we light candles and relax in the aftermath of party, presents, and *poffertjes*—coin-sized Dutch pancakes sprinkled with confectioner's sugar that we traditionally consume at midnight on Christmas Eve. I look out the kitchen window before going to bed to see the bareness and barrenness of winter illuminated by a full moon. Everything has been stripped to its essence. Branch shadows made by the glow of a full moon criss-cross the back clearing's thin frost of snow. Like the ancient Celts, I bow before the moon and wish it good-night.

Frank and I spend a weekend in New York City, where I take myself to the magnificent Morgan Library to see an expansive collection of diaries. I spend a full three hours in the library's special exhibit. My favorites are Thoreau's journals hand-illustrated with exquisite renderings of feathers and leaves. But others are equally as intriguing, including John Steinbeck's daily journal, in which he expresses frustration with his writing progress. He confesses that he's not sure he even wants to keep journals—"time wasters" that they are! He confesses to the page that he would rather be writing novels. Then there is the perfectly preserved illustrated journal of a young soldier at the Battle of Gettysburg. I can't imagine how he found ink and paper, not to mention the presence of mind, to chronicle his experience in that time and place. As I leave the exhibit and walk back toward our hotel, I decide somewhere between 40th and 45th Streets that my dream job would be to oversee the National Museum of American Diaries and Journals. Not that such an organization currently exists under one roof. So many intimate writings and personal chronicles are scattered throughout the country—in church basements, public libraries, universities, private collections, museums, and house attics—but so many have been lost.

Scribbled on unfurled paper coffee cups, dashed on ruled pages of black-and-white-marbled Composition Books, or written by hand in leather-bound journals—words of everyday ordinariness have the power to bring me to my knees. So it is, that on a subsequent weekend trip to Cape Cod's Salt Pond Visitor Center, I am again excited to find an antique journal—the whaling ship diary of Betsey Augusta Penniman. Mrs. Penniman, who accompanied her sea captain husband aboard a whaling vessel in the 1860s, kept a meticulous record of their voyage. Her impeccable penmanship is a linear work of art etched in brown ink. Accompanying her writings are miniature sketches of whales. Gazing through the glass case at her diary, I wished I could release the diary from its hold and read more than the one entry displayed.

How and when does the ordinary act of putting pen to paper become infused with meaning? Do lives become extraordinary only upon their demise? As a child, I read an endless library loop of biographies, all written expressly for children and imbued with 'goody-two-shoes' endings. In disgust with the authors' formulaic accounts that sanctified and sanitized historic individuals, at age nine or ten I closed the cover on yet another saccharine biography of Abigail Adams and declared to anyone within earshot that I wanted to grow up to become a biography teacher about *real* people. I envisioned myself as the future keeper of reverence for everyday experience and ordinary life. Following our trips to New York City and Cape Cod, I am astonished to read in *The New York Times* that an Italian museum constructed around this very idea already exists in a small Tuscan town.

Did we Americans ever love the land? Or did our forebears just want to conquer and control it? Artists of the New York Hudson River School of Painting certainly loved the land, which they considered a spiritual wellspring. Their panoramic views of waterfalls and immense mountain peaks convey nature as all powerful and sacred. In the late 1860s, the German painter Albert Bierstadt could not get enough of our vast, spiritually-charged landscape. Neither could an increasing number of other European artists who left off painting Greek temples and Italianate ruins to find inspiration in the wilds of the North American continent. These painters perceived that Americans were defined by their relationship with the land. I'm wondering if they would still come to this conclusion were they to reappear to paint the woodlands and wetlands edging our neighborhood, where I pick up discarded beer and wine bottles, Dunkin' Donuts coffee cups, plastic straws, and other trash tossed out car windows. I am heartened by the efforts of a woman in the nearby town of Newbury who worked with carpentry students to construct a 12-foot transparent structure to house the staggering amount of litter collected around her small New England community on a regular basis. The structure—known as the Trash Tower—is prominently displayed at the town's elementary school so that all who pass by will see and, in seeing, will think about the wonder of the earth and our collective disrespect and destruction of it. I have decided to create a new category in my mind called "Earth Angels." For now, the woman who spearheaded the idea for the Trash Tower has pride of place. She is precisely the type of person who should be celebrated—extraordinarily ordinary.

An entire cabinet in my kitchen is full of empty jars: Squat mustard jars, skinny olive jars, wide-mouthed pickle jars, and tiny jam jars from hotel breakfast rooms—my favorite. It pleases me no end to have found an artistic use for these cast-offs. I fill them with miniature pine cones, shards of sea glass, dried flowers, twigs, shells, stones, pine needles, and acorns, and line my window sills with these tiny tableaux. They are miniature worlds unto themselves. The fact that they are rapidly taking over our windows suggests to me that I have to find some way to disperse them to an appreciative consumer base. I am thinking about labeling them 'Mother Nature in a Jar' and assembling them on a board at the end of our drive for neighborhood children to find during bicycle forays up and down the street. Perhaps I could use my marketing savvy to suggest them as the perfect Mother's Day gift. What mother wouldn't be delighted to find vestiges of Mother Earth on her breakfast tray along with burned toast and weak coffee? I suspect that the three enterprising blonde girls, who sell their small Giacometti-like tin-foil sculptures at a "store" set up at the end of their drive, will be especially intrigued. Perhaps their mother will receive a trinity of miniature nature tableaux on her breakfast tray.

Every once in a while, as I putter about my kitchen, I have vague intimations of my own mother. She is wearing a homemade, cotton apron edged in rick-rack over a blouse and wrap-around dungaree skirt—her 1960s housewife uniform. Oddly enough, I feel the presence of my maternal grandmother accompanying her. I can't imagine why. Overwhelmed by the Jet Age (not to mention the Space Age), neither of my mother's parents ever worked up the temerity to leave their tiny town in Minnesota and visit us on the East Coast, not even when their only daughter was beset by too many children and the onset of a lingering, life-threatening illness. "I'll never go east of the Mississippi," her younger brother pronounced when my mother married my father and headed east to escape the confines of corn fields and the aisles of her father's dry goods store. Apparently, neither would her parents. After all, people have their barriers and boundaries.

In a flight of fancy, I imagine that, if my mother were to manifest as anything other than herself, she would appear as a tall, stately stem of foxglove. Not because she was particularly tall and stately, but because foxglove is the source for digitalis, the heart ailment prescription she took for years. Not being a gardener, I had no idea what foxglove looked like until one enormous, lone trumpeting stem sprouted at the edge of my fledgling woodland garden. I scoured botany websites to find out what this most impressive plant could be until I happened upon a picture of foxglove and was stunned to discover its connection to digitalis.

All artists know that boundaries between worlds are porous. Contemporary composer John Luther Adams writes musical compositions that erase boundaries in nature. Oceans, rivers, deserts, and mountains become musical scores. Through sound, Adams creates a sense of place and invites listeners in to experience and explore. In doing so, listeners' barriers are breached. They leave their own compartmental worlds to become one with the sea or breezes among pines. Theologian Miroslav Volf uses a musical analogy to explain this same erasure of boundaries in time. He suggests that the present is like a cello string. The here and now is not locked inside a block of impermeable, compartmentalized time, but resonates with the arc of the past as well as the future. Everything blurs. Everything resonates. It is not difficult for me to embrace this notion, since the pattern I live by is not linear, but circular: Birth—death—resurrection, all happening at any one time. It's forwards and backwards, round and round simultaneously. When does birth stop and death begin? When does death stop and resurrection begin? How many angels dance on the head of a pin?

Chapter 5

The Listening Post

On a frigid Sunday morning, I light a fire in the study and assemble thick slices of homemade wheat toast spread with local honey and marmalade. I make a pot of black tea, boil eggs, and slice oranges. It is 17 degrees Fahrenheit—with a wind chill of zero. There's no point, or reason, to brave such weather. I am restless in this house-bound state and decide to clean out the basement. In doing so, I unearth a serendipitous find: A needlework sampler of woodland animals that my sister Sally had mail-ordered from a cereal company and stitched decades ago. For a couple of box tops and a dollar or two, she unwittingly secured the perfect homespun work of art for my woodland shed. Not only are the colorful little creatures perfectly themed to fit into the shed's surroundings, the sampler's expression of our transitory nature is more than appropriate to ponder as I ruminate in my shed: *I shall pass this way but once, therefore any good that I can do or any kindness that I can show, let me do it now, for I shall not pass this way again.* I remove the sampler from its rickety, old frame, wash it in cold water, and take it to a framer in Newburyport, who professionally reframes it and sets it in his storefront display window for passersby to ponder until I arrive to pick it up.

I take advantage of this enforced work suspension on my shed to read about how I might apply the harmonizing principles of *feng shui* to its interior design. I discover that transitional spaces serve an important function to an edifice. Apparently, it is not advisable to construct a dwelling wherein the front door opens directly into one's primary living space. It's far too abrupt. There's transitioning to be done, a shedding of the outer world, and a welcoming into the structure's embrace. My shed's transitional space—the space where I will be shedding the outer world—will be a series of three wooden steps up to its threshold. I analyze instructions and diagrams I find in home construction magazines for how to build steps during the final component of my shed-building project come spring.

We take turns where we build our fire—study by morning, family room in the evening. It's not that we need the fires' heat. After all, our 1978 Gambrel Colonial is outfitted with a 250-gallon oil tank and furnace. It's not a fire's physical warmth we crave so much as the fire's presence, the one that curls and rises into puffs of smoke the minute I strike match to newspaper. I wonder at the supposed allure of a fake fire wiggling away on a television screen in New England pubs at this time of year. The image is there, distorted as it is, but the fire's presence is not. It's like battery-operated "fire-safe" candles. You may as well turn on the lights and be done with it.

A solo drive home from Boston during a sudden and violent snowstorm is treacherous. Sitting behind the wheel, I—stalled and stupefied—watch snow pile up alongside the roads leading north toward I-93. Finally onto the highway I crawl, where massive tractor trailers are stuck on gentle inclines and cars are fishtailing. Lane markers are obliterated in the white-out. I bless the truck in front of me as I follow along behind, keeping my tires in its tire tracks and using the red lights outlining its top corners as guides in the dark and swirling snow. It takes me more than four hours to drive 28 miles. I arrive at the end of our drive to find Tyler and a friend snow-blowing and digging out a path for me to get the car up and into the garage. "Mom! The car looks like it's been through a war!" Tyler shouts as I uncurl my fingers from the steering wheel and haul myself out of the driver's seat. I survey the icicles clinging to the sides of the car and growing along the hood and headlights. I see chunks of snow triangulated behind the front tires. Is it possible to love a car? I wanted to pat it, rub it down, tell it "good car," breathe words of gratitude into its ear, offer it water. Instead, I shut the garage door and leave it to its own devices as I take myself off to a hot bath followed by a dinner of tomato soup and saltines.

Snow and brutal temperatures make a soak in the hot tub off our back deck a distinct pleasure. On Friday nights, Frank and I wrap in beach towels and carry candles out to the tub. Our bare feet skitter along the frozen decking. The colder and snowier it is, the better the water feels. Clouds of steam bellow upwards, eddying about our heads before dissipating in the night sky. Candle flames dance side to side in Mason jars while overarching branches creak back and forth in the wind. Entire trees lean in to share confidences with us and eavesdrop on ours. It is such a gift—this opportunity to stargaze in the middle of winter's frigid temperatures while immersed in soothing hot water.

Overnight, snow falls and falls and falls, until all schools and some work places are closed the following day, including mine. I put on my cross-country skis to cut a short trail through the perimeter of the Audubon sanctuary at the end of our street, but then go deeper into the woods when our neighbor Paula comes along with the same idea. The two of us take off through arches of snow-laden pines and head up and over the beaver lodge at the isthmus, where we spy beaver trails in a ridge of flattened snow.

I walk out across the snow to visit my shed in morning's soft light and see crisscrossing rows of animal tracks. Mice leave a long, thin tail trail between the imprint of their tiny feet. Squirrel tracks— two larger in the back and two smaller up front—look like four miniature mittens pressed into the snow. Deer tracks are sharp and pointy, evidence of unrestrained prancing and pirouetting. The animals have visited under cover of darkness. Despite the fact that I followed the shed company's instructions to buy sharp-edged gravel—supposed deterrents for burrowing ground creatures—for the drainage foundation of my shed, I notice rabbit and mice tracks disappearing into the small space under my studio.

Mollie taught me to see the hidden world at work, to observe its tiny and all-but-invisible activities. I took note of her infinite patience as she lay in wait for chipmunks along the low stone wall that separates our house from our neighbor's. I observed her fine focus as she lay, watchful and alert to the movements and sounds of birds, splayed out on the front porch. She was sometimes so still that butterflies or dragonflies would startle her by landing on her head or front paws. I think about sitting down next to her on the porch steps, resting my hand on her soft, square head and looking intently with her, quietly observing the sounds, the smells, the sights along our front brick walkway that gives way to voluminous rhododendron bushes. I want to tell her about the birds that recently came swooping and hopping and fluttering in from the ravine to find scattered heels of bread I had tossed out onto the snow. Orioles, woodpeckers, starlings, wrens, and sparrows—somehow all received word of the feast. I watched them fly up along the frozen laundry line, hop along the benches on the back deck, land on the old café table, and cock their small feathered heads this way and that. Each one flew off with crumbs in its beak toward winter's late afternoon light. It reminded me of the sunny spring day decades before, when I had cut Frank's hair outside, mindlessly tossing his thick black curls to the ground. The birds swooped in greedily, fluttering and hopping all around our feet, to get the most comfortable and warm material imaginable for their nests. It took us by surprise that birds should be so bold, and made us laugh to see Frank's discarded curls coveted and carried away in their tiny feet.

With Mollie no longer here, animals from the ravine are bolder than ever. They creep out of the underbrush, amble down the back rise, sun themselves on our deck. Woodchucks, fox, fishers, rabbits, squirrels, deer, turtles, snakes. Our yard is now their domain, a regular menagerie. I keep waiting for deer to investigate my shed now that it's in place. I watch and wait, but, as of yet, none have ambled in from the back rise or ravine during daytime hours to see what's going on near their run.

🍃 🍃 🍃

We spend New Year's Eve stirring wedges of Emmentaler and Gruyere into a creamy fondue for the four of us. The square kitchen island offers a perfect fondue venue; each seat is within easy dipping distance of the pot. It's the one meal of the year that we always made together and, for now, we still do. Bethany cuts up a baguette and assembles mushrooms and broccoli heads for dipping. Tyler sets the table and pours drinks. I toss together a garden salad while Frank hovers over the stove, keeping the amount of white wine, garlic, and cheese melting into perfection. Afterwards, the kids go off to their own merry-making with friends while Frank and I head north to make our way along Rockport's wind-blown narrow streets as we migrate from one entertainment venue to another. It's the town's "First Night" celebration; live musicians, magicians, and other performers give us an excuse to buy noise-makers and plastic beaded necklaces. Rockport in winter is about as frigid as any tiny New England hamlet can be, what with the great pulsating ocean hurling itself up against the town wharves and fierce gales blowing in off the troughs of waves. The kiddie programs start at six, but since we no longer have "kiddies," we don't arrive until nine or 10, when our favorite performers begin. The Stuart Highlanders Pipe Band makes a grand entrance into the town's high-ceilinged Congregational Church, where one wall plaque after another recounts the parish's involvement in historic events. But history plays second fiddle on New Year's Eve when pipers, decked out in tartans and tassels, process smartly up the aisle of the church in the wake of a kilted drummer. Two melodies, one right after the other, explode from instruments traditionally fashioned from calf skin. Great bellowing notes of "Amazing Grace" and "Auld Lang Syne" shimmy up the walls and shake us down to our shoes. Frank and I sit close enough to the performance so that I notice earplugs tucked inside the pipers' ears. Apparently, there's only so much bellowing and moaning even a bagpiper can stand. Every year, I insist on attending the piping, and every year I conclude that bagpipes are meant to be played outdoors, preferably in the Scottish Highlands where the great and mournful bleating can rise up and away into mantles of mist.

We recuperate by heading to other venues featuring a New Orleans Jazz Band and something called the "60s Invasion"—a group that performs signature songs of various rock bands of that era. The Beatles' melodies are by far the favorite. Frank and I belt out the lyrics to "I Want to Hold Your Hand" and "Please Please Me" along with the performers and everyone else in the audience. Just before midnight, we stop off at two powerful telescopes set up by the Gloucester Astronomy Club in Dock Square. The minute I put eye to glass, I go weak in the knees. The entire reality of space— the VOID—has always overwhelmed me. To distract myself from errant existential thoughts, I concentrate on how close the moon appears. If my arm were a little longer, I could touch the shores of the Sea of Tranquility. On this New Year's Eve, in a cloudless, crystal sky, the moon is afloat in a black abyss before my eyes. I stagger away from the telescope and reorient myself on this planet by grabbing Frank's hand and joining the crowd streaming toward the town Christmas tree. For a few minutes at the stroke of midnight, there are no strangers in Rockport, only mittened hands holding mittened hands, forming a chain around a pine tree festooned with rainbow lights and seashell ornaments. All of us—our breath floating up and over our faces in the frigid night air—belt out the ancient lamentation of old and lost acquaintances while the earth hangs in its galaxy and moonbeams grace our world.

During some New England winters, I could swear we were living at the North Pole. Others are so mild that I cannot make sense of it. But this is a year of snows. After the biggest storm so far, Tyler, home from college for a mid-winter visit, builds an igloo at the edge of the drive. The snow is compact and heavy. When piles of it split away in chunks, an iridescent turquoise light glows from the fissures, as if the flakes had absorbed heaven's light during their fall to earth. At dusk, Bethany—who also happens to be visiting—and I light three small candles in Mason jars, and take them out to Ty's igloo. All three of us lean in and sit cross-legged on the snow floor, the igloo's rounded walls winking and sparkling in candlelight as our breath vaporizes and encircles our heads.

Frank and I feel desperate to get away. To recover from a sore throat (me), root canal (Frank), and just plain boredom this winter (all of us in New England suffering through unending storms), we need to do something. On the philosophy of "if you can't beat 'em, join 'em," we decide to head up to the Trapp Family Lodge in Stowe, Vermont. "Bring your cross-country skis," says the reservation agent when I call to book a room. "Conditions are pristine."

When we arrive, it is snowing to beat the band. As our headlights sweep across snow banks in front of the lodge, thousands of iridescent crystals explode in a miniature light show. The next day, flakes—individual and fluffy and distinct—continue falling at a steady clip, providing a layer of powder for our cross-country runs. As we *shuss* across snow-covered meadows and groomed trails through the woods, the earthy scent of wood smoke surrounds the Tyrolean-style lodge. We ski across fields to the cozy Viennese Tea Room for a lunch of mushroom soup and hot potato salad, not to mention an array of sinful desserts. It's tortes, tarts, *kuchen* and strudel. It's gliding through covered wooden bridges and passing by iced-over streams. It's encountering traditional Austrian religious shrines of wooden crucifixes protected by pointy wooden roofs at various intervals along the trails. It's long, gentle runs through pine forests toward the Von Trapp family cemetery where Baron Georg Von Trapp and several of his children who also escaped Nazi-controlled Austria are buried. It's a slice of *The Sound of Music.* That evening, Frank and I sip peppermint schnapps and hot chocolate in front of the lodge's roaring fire.

"Is it all a bit much?" Frank asks, gesturing toward the pianist playing "Climb Every Mountain" and the wait staff dressed in *lederhosen.*

"Live it up," I say. "We've got Austria at our doorstep for a fraction of what it costs to actually go there."

The morning following our return from Vermont, I gaze forlornly out the kitchen window to the large, rounded snow hump that is my shed. I'm stuck. I can't seem to embark on the next stage of construction. The cold temperatures and piles of snow are good enough reasons to feel daunted by the task. Another is that I don't know what kind of insulation to buy or how to get the huge sheets home in my small car. Nor do I have the confidence to install it. At age 70-something, Marilyn takes charge. In the last 20 years, she has constructed two pottery sheds and two kiln sheds along with a shed for potting plants. In her book, insulation installation is a minor blip in shed construction. She and I drive to Ipswich to buy sheets of insulation at a local lumber and hardware store. Marilyn refuses to do business with chain building-supply stores housed in structures the size of airplane hangars. I see the logic of this the minute we receive the undivided attention of two Tedford's Lumber employees. The storage area is full of sheets of insulation with as many different "R" factors as there are letters in the alphabet. Marilyn knows exactly what to buy and how to have it cut so that it fits in the back of her station wagon, and she makes no bones about sharing her hard-earned knowledge of construction, not to mention her car's dimensions, with the young men helping us. Once we get back and haul the awkward, unwieldy sheets of insulation from car to shed, we measure the areas between the wall studs and begin scoring the insulation sheets to fit. It's a giant jigsaw puzzle. Cutting and fitting the foam pieces into place suddenly feels like child's play! All it takes is a measuring tape, a sharp-edged razor, and patience.

"I told you this would be fun," Marilyn says, as she measures everything three times. She doesn't want me to have to go back and trim off edges. "Measure thrice and cut once," she warns.

I love that she uses an old-fashioned word like thrice. We run out of insulation before the end of the afternoon, so Frank and I return to Tedford's the next morning for two more sheets. By the end of the weekend, the walls of my Bird's Nest are insulated. I'm not sure if this amount of insulation will suffice, or if I'll have to insulate the ceiling, too. I'm willing to experiment a season to see how warm and snug my shed is before I take on the pitched roof area. I like the ceiling's open beams.

It's a gentle fairy snow that's falling in the morning the first time I write inside my shed. I am warm enough inside its newly insulated interior as long as I wear my down coat, but my fingers holding the pen begin to cramp and complain. It's time to stop. I only stay long enough to write two words in my journal: Waxing and waning. Like realm and dwell, they are suggestive of other worlds, and I want to remember them here on the edge of the ravine.

"I wish to speak a word for Nature," Henry David Thoreau wrote as the preamble to his essay "Walking." *I wish to speak a word for Nature.* During an afternoon outing to Concord Public Library's special collections, I hold Thoreau's original "Walking" manuscript in my hands. My throat closes up tight and my eyes start to swim when I see the mottled brown ink on the page, his flourishing, spidery penmanship. I note that he crossed out "this evening" in the first sentence. Maybe he was not sure if he was going to deliver the essay as a lecture in the evening, or in the afternoon. Perhaps he felt the phrase diminished the drama of his opening line. He did not wish to speak *this evening* for Nature; he simply wanted to speak *a word* for Nature—as in always. I keep reading. I see a paragraph circled and x'd out. A century and a half after his hand recorded his thoughts and revised his first impulses, Thoreau's mind modulates across the page in front of me. His spindly-legged writing desk inside nearby Concord Museum did not convey his presence to me the way this original document does. I feel his energy and ideas—his essence and presence—between the lines. I also begin to feel the presence of a librarian hovering discreetly in my vicinity as I peruse this literary treasure and original source document. My time is up. I must relinquish Thoreau to the shelves of the Concord Library archives.

The Bird's Nest is every bit the listening post I want it to be. Even if I do nothing more than sweep my binoculars across piles of barren mud and snow lumped together at the bottom of the ravine, I leave ordinariness behind when I step across its threshold. All is shot through, as Jesuit poet Gerard Manley Hopkins wrote, "with the grandeur of God." I am aware of an underlying feeling of anticipation, though what I am listening or waiting for remains a mystery. Like shepherds of old, I am abiding. What a primitive sense of comfort this is. What a refuge. Bundled inside my down coat, I revel in solitude and silence.

I go walking in the Audubon sanctuary at the end of our street and spot what appear to be slender tree trunks in a thicket of pine. The sheen of the trunks prompts me to look closer. They are not trunks at all, of course. That's when I raise my gaze to lock eyes with a full-grown doe. Something passes between us that I cannot fathom. I fall into a type of removed consciousness while receiving the deer's energy, its life force, its intelligence and singular focus. I am entranced. I wonder what it receives from me during the exchange. I wait for the doe to break its gaze, but it seems it can stare at me forever. I am the first to look away. This seems to be the way of the wild. During my encounter with the frog in the ravine and another time with an owl during a walk in the woods with Mollie, I had to be the one to look away.

It's the shoulder season, and Frank and I have signed up for a tour of the maple sugaring process, otherwise known as "sugaring off," at the Audubon sanctuary. As we pick our way toward the specially prepared sugar shack, our boots alternately sink and slurp into murky brown slush and slide in snow up to our shins. The scent of wood smoke intermingling with a slight sweetness hovers in the raw breeze. Before we are allowed to enter the shack, we must listen to the story of the sugar maples and how they are tapped. A little girl named Emily serves as our group's prototype of a sugar maple. Our guide zips out a measuring tape to assess the circumference of Emily's small waist and tells her that she has been officially approved for tapping since her "trunk" measures the minimally required ten inches. That means, he says, that Emily is 40 years old in tree years. Emily smiles. She is clearly delighted to be the star of the "sugaring off" show.

We discover that the transformation of a tree's lifeblood into liquid candy is a matter of degree. Alternating warming and cooling temperatures provoke the sap's movement inside the tree, causing it to rise up into the tree's trunk and branches by day and back down into the roots by night. It's a lot of coming and going, upping and downing. On its way up and down, it finds its way to the bored hole in the tree trunk and drip-drops into a steel bucket positioned beneath the spout, otherwise known as a spile, inserted into the trunk. When it's our turn to finally enter the sugar shack, we are stunned by the heat. The log-fed fire underneath the evaporator bins is the workhorse of the operation, turning sap into syrup through the distribution of heat. We learn that a substance composed of 97 percent water and three percent sugar has to be boiled at a temperature of 219 degrees Fahrenheit to transform it into a substance of 66 percent sugar and 33 percent water. There is magic in numbers. Sap turns into syrup. For $6, we take home a maple-leaf-shaped jar full of the amber-colored liquid. That evening, in front of the fire, Frank and I eat dessert for dinner. I fry up buttery crepes and roll them with cinnamon and apples drizzled with syrup.

The temperate air doesn't last long. We wake the next day to find our bedroom windows covered in ice pictures. The crystals look like tiny forests of albino ferns. Others resemble flocks of miniature doves on the wing. My favorite is the pattern that suggests dancing stars. It is art that arrives silently in the middle of the night and brings me surprised delight in the morning. There must be some correlation between our body heat and the appearance of window frost. When Frank is away on business, my breath barely results in a tiny flock of crystal birds on one corner of the window nearest our bed. When he's home, both bedroom windows are completely covered in ice art, so that when the morning sun slants across the crystals, the room becomes iridescent with sparkly light.

Halibut Point, along Rockport's coast, is a great jagged plateau of granite boulders tossed and jumbled at a point of land looking out toward the Isles of Shoals. The North Atlantic appears to stretch into eternity from these rocky outcroppings. During World War II, the government built a concrete watchtower here for scouts to scan the waves in search of enemy submarines. But we have come in search of harbor seals that have recently been reported in these waters. We think we might see them roll right up and over in the curl of heavy surf—arcs of white spray with emerald green underbellies. We scan the swells for whiskered faces, for buoyant brown or gray bodies, but we don't see a single one. It's too cold on the exposed cliffs to stay for very long. We turn to go as the sinking sun draws a dark cape up along the throat of the land. It's time for home, where I take a thermos of tea out to The Bird's Nest to write by the glow of a Coleman Lantern and breathe in the scent of pine boards and ceiling joists. I wonder when the peepers will begin cranking up their throaty trilling to tell us that spring is here.

It's 71 degrees on the day after St. Patrick's Day. Impossible! New England is rarely this warm at this time of year. A full sun melts my raspberry ice cream as I linger at White Farms Ice Cream stand on the Rowley/Ipswich border. The bare treetops bend and wave in high winds. I am drowsy and delirious with sunshine. The fly buzzing around my purse is as well. It flies in weird little loop-de-loops, occasionally landing on my purse zipper to get its bearings. Both of us are drunk with sunshine. I tilt my face upward to the sun and notice that there is only one dirt-crusted snow mound in sight. Alleluia! I chomp on my sugar cone until it is a tiny triangular nub, which, I am reminded, always used to be Mollie's special treat. I pop the final bit into my mouth to be done with it. There will be no grieving my good girl gone on this bountiful, beautiful day.

The Bird's Nest warms up nicely in the spring sunshine, so much so that I crank open the awning, or wing, window to let in the freshening air. The ice on the vernal pond has almost fully receded. At one point, I hear the glug-glugging of amphibians—music to my ears! It's a mud bath walking from the back deck to my shed. I have to wear rubber boots to get across the muck. On my way to and from The Bird's Nest, I notice that Miss Crab Apple is perking up. She must be happier now that she is coming into her flowering season. Looking down into the dead wood and leaf mess on the forest floor of the ravine, I see lustrous patches of brilliant green moss throbbing in triangles of sunlight. I briefly consider clearing a path into this sodden world, but think better of it. I have intervened enough.

Chapter 6
All the Questions and Answers of the Universe

On a Sunday afternoon at the end of March, Frank and I arrive at the northern tip of Plum Island to find a fierce current running out the Merrimack River to the Atlantic. The red marker at the entrance to the channel is bent sideways, straining toward the open ocean. Once again, we are in search of seals. Without binoculars, I would not have spied them lounging on rocks at the mouth of the river. The seals are gray and bulbous, their upturned bellies white, which makes it easy enough to distinguish them from their black rocky beds. The creatures are great lumps of gray mass, nothing like the frisky be-whiskered seals at the Boston Aquarium that slide and glide at amazing speed through water visible through a thick transparent wall. They don't appear to be anything like the cigar-shaped seal I encountered sunning itself on Crane Beach either. According to the volunteer at the nature center on the way over to Plum Island, it's starting to be too warm for seals around these parts. Apparently, 40-degree water feels like a steam bath to arctic seals. They are all migrating north to the frigid waters of Hudson Bay, which is how we have come to see so many in one day.

Plum Island is part of the barrier island chain that stretches from New England to the Carolinas. Among its dunes, I find great gnarled pieces of driftwood as we push our way back to the parking lot through a bitter wind, and I stop to collect one or two smaller pieces for mobiles I construct from the worn, twisted shapes. The beach is littered with other debris as well. There are cracked Solo cups left over from summer picnics, a key ring, a disintegrating shoe, a plastic fork with tines pointing upward from the sand—a paltry facsimile of Neptune's trident. The thought occurs to me that there is no place for plastic in nature. Its very presence violates. I worry about the piping plovers that will make their nests among trash in the sea grasses and sandy troughs.

Winter is not going gently into that good night. Even though we are on the cusp of spring, we get another dumping of snow. It's shoulder-season snow, heavy with water and not the best for snow sports. Still, in hopes of getting in a last ski or two, I take myself to

Appleton Farms for what turns out to be an aborted 20-minute run through the gloppiest snow of the season. On the way home, I make up for the less than pristine conditions by detouring to Zumis Coffee Shop, where I sit at a window table to down a frothy cappuccino and watch wet snowflakes fly sideways across the street. Inside, I glory in the deep earth-drenched scent of freshly ground coffee beans and classical guitar music from sunny Spain playing over the sound system. And I chat with Umesh, Zumis' owner, who greets me with his palms pressed together as if in prayer and with a slight bow says, "*Namaste*. How are you today?"

It hardly feels like Eastertide. I wear hat and gloves and my heaviest woolen coat to the Holy Thursday evening service at the Congregational Church of Topsfield. I, along with other assembled worshipers in the spare meeting house, listen to the story of Jesus breaking bread at his last supper in full knowledge of what awaited him. One by one, the lights are dimmed in mourning for his coming betrayal and crucifixion. As the last light is dimmed, the nave falls into complete darkness, except for the illumination of one large white candle that the minister lifts high as we all silently leave our pews and process outside. "Stay with me. Remain with me. Watch and pray. Watch and pray." We worshipers chant the simple tune in unison until we congregate on the icy walkway and go our separate ways. The steeple's bell tolls across the town common which, at this hour, is hushed and wrapped in the dark chill of night. The tolling bell shudders through my bones. Above, sharp, glittering-blue stars burn in a blue-black sky. On this night, all is silent except for the clear and ponderous toll of the bell: *"Watch and pray."*

On Easter Sunday, I am surrounded by elderly women. They amass either by themselves or accompanied by a friend, perhaps a caretaker, who assists with a walker and a supporting hand. In ones and twos they arrive in church. Their short, white hair is thinning and fly-away, their lips dabbed a bright coral or red. Some are younger elders, trendier, with bobbed stylish haircuts, silver hoops in their ears, high heels on their feet. Others exhibit a worn fragility, and wear orthotic shoes. Mostly, I observe their solitary dignity. Despite their frailty, they all exhibit such fortitude and endurance. I wonder how many self iterations each of them has passed through. Every single woman has unearthed a touch of Easter purple from her closet—a lavender sweater set, an aubergine-striped scarf, a jaunty eggplant-colored hat. All are swathed in the color of the resurrection. I glance down and congratulate myself on my own choice of fashion. Suede purple pumps have carried me into their good and gracious company.

Two snowdrops have emerged at the base of the back deck. The day after the frozen variety has finally disappeared from every shady corner of our yard, I spy the flowers' dainty, droopy heads.

"Chin up!" I say, as I lift their tiny faces to the sun. "It's spring!" But, no. Back down on slender stalks their chins go. It's as if they have used up all their energy just to poke up out of the near-frozen ground and don't have an ounce in reserve.

That we can grasp the reality of great friends on a moment skipping by is a truth I live by. Suddenly, there is Charlene, whom I have been assigned to interview for an article. I am sitting on a concrete bench in the sun at our appointed time and place as I cast my eyes across strangers coming and going. Having never met Charlene, I am uncertain as to who my interviewee could be. A tiny woman with short graying hair goes rushing by, only to turn around and come darting back toward me. Everything about her movements reminds me of a bird. "Are you Charlene?" I ask. Talking to Charlene is like talking to another version of myself. I have apparently—but unbeknownst to me—known her all my life. Such a richly textured personality! I see that she is a traveler, writer, entrepreneur, seeker of a better way, thinker, and pilgrim. In fact, she tells me that her thesis for graduation from divinity school is focused on "Pilgrimage and Divinity." By the end of our interview, which turns into a complex and convoluted conversation, we are exchanging phone numbers and email addresses. She is as surprised to find me as I am to find her. "I think we're connected," she says before we say our good-byes. "Don't you?"

Meeting Charlene reminds me that, if we can lose those we love in a skip of a second, we can also find them. As an older adult, making deep and solid friendships can be elusive, a real challenge. I note that finding those who can and want to offer a level of relationship that brings a richness of feeling and shared experience of exploration and creativity takes work—and more than a little luck. Most people I encounter on a daily basis rely on acceptable rules of conversation, a prescription for predictable relationship. There is, of course, some comfort in this, but also less-than-interesting interactions. I remind myself routinely that other people are not here to entertain or enrich me in some way. But what a gift it is when a sympathetic and spontaneous soul appears to expand my world.

There are days when I can't imagine why I ever wanted a house on the ocean. There is plenty of water in Topsfield. The spring peepers, toads, and wood frogs gulp and sing their slimy little hearts out in its wetlands and vernal pools from late afternoon until well into the night. As I head out on my bike, pedal past the marshlands, and swing along back roads into downtown Topsfield, the air vibrates with high-pitched chirping and whirring and humming. Their singing animates everything. It is constant chatter in the background of daily doings. The amphibians age and proliferate; their voices get deeper and louder. As they crank up they sound like a chorus of out of tune cellos getting ready for a concert. The pitch of their thrumming is deafening. It is a wild, loud trilling that makes me think of vintage black-and-white "Tarzan" movies. We could be in the overgrowth of the Amazon instead of sedate New England. The rubbery, throaty, gulping trilling rises and falls in steep crescendos of orgasmic sound as dusk falls into the deepening dark. I think we are lucky to live next door to their raucous presence, our house with a "water view" of a vernal pond.

Still, I go to the ocean as a matter of course, no matter the season. Once I hear that rain is forecast for the next few days, I take myself out for an evening amble at the edge of Crane Beach while I wait for Frank to come home from work. The sky meets the horizon in a watercolor wash of baby blue—the exact color of my jacket. I could be part of the horizon if it asked me to. It is just about all pale blue, with one faint stripe of pearly pink. Several sandbars are exposed, their fingers pointing out toward the sea. Small waves lap the beach at an angle and make a gulping, gurgling sound. The piping plovers, tiny frenetic birds that make astoundingly symmetrical patterns in the sky, twitter and skitter in groups at the water's edge. Their spindly toothpick legs are marvels of engineering. Their feverish level of activity and singularity of purpose remind me of myself.

Now that spring is finally here and fine weather is allowing me to finish my shed in earnest, I am trying not to feel overwhelmed. I make a list of tasks for myself:

- Hang and stain interior paneling;

- Hang shelving;

- Construct steps up into shed;

- Install screens in my "foundling" Andersen windows;

- Affix decorative tiles over the door;

- Install lattice around the foundation;

- Assemble interior decorations and wall hangings;

- Design and plant a simple rock garden and grotto on the side of the shed away from the ravine.

My first job is to panel over the shed's exposed interior insulation. That means I need pine paneling cut to fit, which I shop for at the nearest mega construction store. Despite Marilyn's misgivings and ample warnings about poor customer service in enormous warehouse-type stores, I receive immediate attention from a young sales associate, whose gigantic forearms are covered in scriptural tattoos. Chapter and verse ripple across his biceps as he hoists my four-by-eight-foot sheets of paneling into the jaws of the store's massive cutting machine. I try not to stare as he measures and cuts pieces to fit my shed's dimensions. I deduce that one of his forearms is marked with the year of his birth as well as his year of personal salvation: "Est. 1977, Saved 2009." His biblical tattoos include "Job 13:15," "Philippians 1:21," and "John 18:36." I manage to restrain myself from fishing out the tiny *New Testament* that lives at the bottom of my purse. Instead, I jot chapter and verse surreptitiously on the back of my shopping list to look up later.

Together, we steer the oversized cart loaded with pine paneling up to the cashier desk. That's when I work up the courage to ask him about his devotion to the Word.

"Each reference corresponds to a hurdle I've overcome," he says casually, as if he has forgotten that his muscular physique is a walking-talking scriptural billboard. "I'm a believer."

I nod reverently in the direction of his biceps. "I can see that," I say. "You are definitely marked for life."

Buying pine paneling is one thing. Installing it is another. It takes me 25 to 30 hammer whacks to drive a nail into both paneling and supporting studs. Again, it is a giant jigsaw puzzle lining paneling pieces up with the top and bottom beams as well as the intermittent vertical studs staggered along the shed's interior walls. There are windows and corners to accommodate. Frank tells me that a professional carpenter can whack a nail home in two hits, three at the most. I dismiss this. I will hit a nail a hundred times—carefully, gently, and slowly—if it means that I will avoid banging the tip of my finger with the hammer again. Despite my bruised fingernail, I am making great progress in my shed. Sometimes, I wile away an entire 15 minutes just sitting and staring at what I have accomplished. Perhaps, when I'm done, my fingers will stop throbbing long enough for me to exchange hammer for pen. What do I want to write about? The numinous quality of nature. The everyday observations of taking delight in being alive. To paraphrase 20th-century Canadian artist Emily Carr, I want to write about the hidden thing beneath the surface that "…is felt rather than seen, the reality…which underlies everything."

It's my birthday—a beautiful, sunny day for applying more mushroom-tinted stain to the shed's exterior. I spend a few hours doing that before I grow tired of climbing up and down ladders. I take the afternoon off from manual labor to shop the wildly colorful fabrics and ceramics of Pier I, where I find a perfect indoor/outdoor rug for my shed, along with a wicker chair to place in the corner for visitors. Both the chair and the rug are spicy red. The rug has flecks of ivory and an ivory-colored edge. Perfect! A deep earth-toned red is apparently going to be the complementary color of my decorating accessories. It's a pleasing interplay of color, especially juxtaposed with the shed's mushroom-colored exterior and the white, window-paned door.

I stop by the Sisters' Cuvilly Arts & Earth Center—named after the French birthplace of the order's foundress—to watch the annual rite of sheep shearing. The Congregation's enormous motherhouse is just up the hill from Cuvilly's barnyard, and, if the wind is right, the Sisters and I (as a member of their support staff) are treated to a cacophony of brays, grunts, shrieks, and bleats as we toil over our computers. On my occasional visits to the barnyard,

Sister Pat, who oversees the pre-school on the property as well as the farm, will hand me a large jar of honey harvested from the farm's beehives. I also generally buy fresh eggs while I'm there, which go for $3 a dozen—a modest amount to pay for such farm-to-table freshness. But today, it's just the sheep shearing I'm after; there are no eggs or honey to be had.

Kevin the sheepshearer leads one sheep at a time from the barn. The others are bleating and "baaing," protesting the turn the day has taken. I know that my colleagues, who have elected to forego the show, are getting an earful up at the motherhouse. Judging from the amount of energy and activity inside the barn, the sheep are clearly ill at ease—until, that is, Kevin sticks his thumb in the corner of each of their mouths. At the touch of thumb to gum, the sheep hit the ground as though Kevin has cast a spell. It's an odd and curious sight to see a protesting and straining animal instantaneously subdued by a thumb. In Kevin's right hand is a pair of shears with oversized curved blades. In mere minutes, he shears—in one perfect, continuous cut—the fleece from the body of a 100-pound border Leicester named Obadiah. There is not one miscalculated cut, not one nick, on Obadiah's shorn skin as the animal staggers up from the ground and is released. The goats and chickens in the barnyard are beside themselves with curiosity. Before the shearing began, every last barnyard creature had been scattered out among pens and paddocks, mucking about and minding their own business. Once Kevin began shearing, the barnyard fell silent, except, that is, for the bleating sheep waiting to be sheared.

I turn to discover Rocco, one of Cuvilly's Sicilian donkeys (uncannily marked, as all Sicilian donkeys are, with a dark-colored cross growing along the length of his spine) expelling his hot breath on the back of my elbow as I observe the show. Sister Pat tells me that Sicilian donkeys are here to remind us of Jesus' ride into Jerusalem on a humble donkey. Rocco appears to be oblivious of his extraordinary physical attribute, not to mention his larger significance in life. He has ambled over to the fence that separates pasture from barnyard to watch the goings-on with the sheep, as do the goats. They all want to know if they are next. I pat Rocco's boney head reassuringly and scratch around his wiry ears.

The Ipswich River—what a gem, a jewel, a beauty in our midst! Overarching ash and oak and pine and maple line the roadway that follows the course of the river between Topsfield and Ipswich. One glorious spring morning as I drive along the road, Bach's "Magnificat" erupts from the radio. Trees, their branches fanning up into the sky, appear to me to be singing, joining in the triumphant swell of brass and choir. I pass from forest to farm houses to open fields along the river. As if to say hello, the "chocolate" horses grazing in the paddock across from Foote Brothers Canoe Rentals lift their heads as I pass. The horses, the overarching branches, the river and rocks, the Passat's recently tuned engine—all are humming and singing in the glory of the day, united by Bach's "Magnificat." I wonder if this is what is meant as cross-sensory perception, or *synaesthesia.* People endowed with this condition see images, colors, or number sequences in response to music or the cadence of poetry. Their minds give rise to one form while experiencing another. What I perceive on this fresh dawn of a morning is the underlying unity of the universe. The sensation of intertwining and inter-penetrating worlds is fleeting, but it is there—as palpable as the wind.

Animals and amphibians glory in the Ipswich River, find their place in it, find life in it, as do I. I frequently ride my bike down Perkins Row in late afternoon sunlight so that I can lean over the old stone bridge across the marshes and watch painted turtles with splashes of yellow and red on their shells sun themselves on the tops of rocks and semi-submerged logs. They know when it's time to haul out of the drink and let themselves bake. There's intelligence in that. I watch a pair swim together through duckweed scattered across the water and poke their heads up for a look around. They decide to go on, spreading out their webbed feet to their impressive full dimension, and swim under the bridge, emerging on the other side. I watch them propel themselves along the current until they disappear into the rushes.

It's odd to think that a river starts anywhere. There are no mountains or lake or spring on the map to explain the origin of the Ipswich River. It simply appears to spring forth from the nondescript exurb of Wilmington before winding its way over and emptying out into Plum Island Sound. It flows through six towns—

Topsfield, being one—before arriving at its terminus in Ipswich Bay. If I could, I would float summer away on a small wooden barge along the Ipswich River, but it's not deep enough and its bridges are not high enough to accommodate anything other than kayaks and canoes. One of my favorite paintings is Claude Monet's "The Studio Boat," and I am lucky enough to see it at a special exhibition at Salem's Peabody Essex Museum. How fortunate was Monet that he could load up this small boat with his paints and float along a river in pastoral France, doing nothing more than painting and sketching and enjoying the flow and feel and scent of water? The life-sized construction of a studio boat inside the museum's exhibit hall includes an audio recording of water lapping against its sides and wooden poles hitting and scraping against its wooden hull, so that as I step inside the fabricated boat I feel as if it is making its way through the current. At the exhibit, I also discover Daubigny, another French artist who created a floating studio for himself and his family and crafted an enchanting book of etchings and sketches of their river voyage called *Voyage en Bateau Croquis a L'Eau Forte* or Boat Trip Sketches in Colored Drypoint. I am, of course, completely taken with his visual journal that has cunning little frogs, marsh grasses, and one tiny dragonfly decorating its cover—sketched by the artist along the riverbanks.

Bethany and I spend an afternoon among the daffodils, violets, and trillium in Marilyn's wooded back yard, searching for what Marilyn considers "seconds" of her exquisite stoneware pottery. Vases and tea cups, plates, candleholders, bowls, and serving dishes are tucked in and among leafy ground cover and rocks adjacent to Marilyn's hillside potting sheds. Deep-green and blue-glazed pots and earth-toned bowls are everywhere. A visit inside her 1920s cottage tells her story: Pottery is spilling off shelves, sitting haphazardly on the stove, stacked by the back door, teetering on dresser tops. This abundance is why Marilyn has scattered what she calls the "lesser of her work" out among her hillside garden and has invited customers and friends for a treasure hunt. She simply has too much of a good thing. Once a year, she must clear the decks so she can continue throwing pots. The proceeds of Marilyn's annual treasure hunt are donated to Rosie's Place, a women's shelter in downtown Boston.

Bethany and I bake bar cookies packed with chocolate and butterscotch chips, walnuts, and coconut. We pack them up and take them with us for Marilyn to serve to her guests. By the time we arrive, everything is already set up. Teapots covered with warming cozies are set on a card table refashioned with rough wooden planks instead of its original Formica laminate. Marilyn has flung a deep-blue woven cloth sideways across its uneven surface and placed platters of sweets on top. A ring of tea cups, each one different in glaze and size from the other, encircles the teapots. Marilyn offers her guests homemade brownies with and without pecans. She has set out a bowl of strawberries still wearing their little green caps.

All of Marilyn's pottery looks at home resting against tree trunks, or looped with twine and hanging from branches, snuggled into a bed of violets, balanced on rocks. "They look so organic," says Bethany, bending over a small tumbler glazed with an image of a dragonfly atop a bed of twigs. "As if they have grown up from the ground," she adds. Which, of course, they have. Their bodies, bottoms, spouts, handles, and finely curved faces and rims are all of clay. They are not meant to be displayed in formal china cabinets or sitting on crocheted white-lace doilies. They are at home on solid wooden fireplace mantles or displayed on a bed of river rocks. As I carefully skirt the trillium on the pottery path, I have a hard time deciding what to add to my burgeoning collection of Marilyn's pottery. In the end, I decide on a mottled blue-glazed vase and two small tumblers. As I write my check, I keep thinking of a mid-size blue-glazed bowl next to a cluster of daffodils. It's not clear if I want the bowl because of how startlingly blue it looks next to the yellow daffodils, or if I really want the bowl. I wait until everyone else has left. If it's unclaimed, then I'm meant to have it. When Bethany and I help Marilyn collect the leftover pots along the path, I see the bowl illuminated by an angle of sunlight. Its blueness calls to me. As I lean down to retrieve it, I see the daffodils nodding. *"You need to have that,"* they say. *"We told you so."*

I walk into Marilyn's hillside garage that she has transformed into a showroom. The cool concrete floor, the stone walls lined with rough wooden planks and cabinets, a worn wooden church pew, and threadbare red-and-blue oriental rugs suggest a chapel or secret cave somewhere in the woods—Bavaria perhaps, or a hidden glen on a

Scottish moor. The pots and vases and teapots pulse with life. It takes less than a second for their syncopated, joyous rhythm to jump into my bones and blood. I feel myself gliding on a burst of energy currents.

"I must tell you," I say to Marilyn, "that your pottery is singing."

She explodes in laughter. "Oh, that's grand!" she says, beaming.

To Marilyn, her pots are alive, and she is delighted that anyone else feels that way. She has named one of her teapots—glazed in shiny black with a handle spiraling upwards in two clasped hands—"Freedom and Bondage." That one, she says, is not for sale. Everyone attending the treasure hunt is given one of her hand-fashioned glazed cups as a party favor.

Here's where I record that things aren't going as smoothly as I would like. The final pieces of paneling I'm trying to fit on the fourth wall of my shed are not coming together as neatly as on the first three. This means the fourth wall is going to be the most "finished" one, with wooden ivy molding trim that I have discovered at a local crafts store covering up my mistakes. I'm on my own. Frank has been a great help up to now, but he has abandoned the paneling project to prepare for the annual spring launch of The Flying Dutchman, his 28-foot sailboat. I have to say "it's a poor trades-woman who blames her tools," but in my case it's not my tools I'm blaming. It's my lack of skill, undeveloped spatial analysis, and dexterity in working with wood. Back and forth I go to the mega home improvement store to buy more paneling pieces to replace the ones I ruin.

If Marilyn's pots are alive, so is my little house. And it's getting impatient. When I step up inside its still unfinished interior, it wants to know when I'll be done already. There are days when I confess to being overwhelmed. I've never tackled such a large project before. The decorative ivy molding is helping me gentle over more gaps and mistakes than I care to admit. I buy yards of it to run up the walls adjacent to the door fame where things have gone slightly awry. I ask my shed if it would like to be called Ivy Cottage instead of The Bird's Nest. It can't decide, and neither can I, but given the yards of ivy molding I'm using to edge its windows and doors, the name seems appropriate. The shed and I are in agreement that everything is taking much longer to finish than I anticipated. Measuring properly to accommodate the mitered corners and then using the miter box to cut and fit the pieces of molding together around the windows is laborious. Surprisingly, it takes a lot of confidence to begin cutting a piece of molding once I've measured it three times, or as Marilyn would say, thrice. I don't like wasting money, or efforts. I am loathe to make mistakes, especially if they are mistakes that could have been avoided by being more careful and deliberate. Are the pieces of molding perfectly joined? No. Do they look terrific as a subtle, lovely finish to the window? Yes. Once I'm satisfied with that end of things, I wash and stain the rough floor planks with a golden oak stain which, at first, I think seems a touch dark. It lightens as it dries, but in doing so it also highlights the flaws of the floor boards where they were patched with wood filler at the factory. As I stand to survey my overall work, I also can't help noticing the one corner of my shed that warps in along the front wall. Frank and I did our best to reinforce it by laying two extra pieces of molding behind the strip of corner molding, along with gobs of "Liquid Nails"—a gooey glue product that rescues untrained carpenters in times of crisis—and some well-placed screws for reinforcement. I begin to feel my inner critic creeping in among the floorboards. It's time to take a break and head into the house for a glass of iced tea. Even though I've left off the project for the day, I can't help gazing at The Bird's Nest from the kitchen window. I love standing at the sink, looking out the window, and seeing the shed's wing window cranked open. It looks as though someone is at home and waiting for me. By the time I head out to work on my shed the next morning, there's no sign of my inner critic. I don't care if my project is "worthwhile" in her eyes, or not. I'm having a marvelous time at play in my shed—and I haven't even finished with its construction yet.

The Bird's Nest is located on a threshold between two worlds. It occupies a liminal space, a place of transition, as do I. That may be why I placed my shed where it is, why I am so drawn to its doorstep. I think of a watercolor painting by Vermont artist Roderick MacIver called "Big Bird." It is of a long-necked heron in flight—wings outstretched—suspended between the round disc of the sun in the sky above and the sun's mirror reflection in the water below. The bird on the wing hangs between the two intersecting worlds, the meeting point for them both.

Once I get the screens installed and the Andersen windows thrown open to the ravine, the noise begins. It's been trying to rain all day, and the wind is whipping itself up into a gale, singing and sighing and whistling through the newly installed screens. I take advantage of the weather to visit the mega home improvement store once again. It takes me three tries, but I finally find stain dark enough for the shed's paneling that will showcase Marilyn's earth-toned owl platter against the back wall. The stain I settle on is aptly named "Ipswich Pine." For the hundredth time, I stand back to admire my shed. It has a presence and identity all its own. We are going to be great and silent friends, my shed and I.

Along comes a ping-pong weekend. One day, we build a fire in the family room and wrap up in woolen blankets as we watch the Boston Bruins battle their way toward the Stanley Cup from the comfort of our couch. The next day dawns humid and hot and foggy;

it's suddenly 80 degrees. We unearth sandals and cotton shirts, turn on ceiling fans. We drive up to York Harbor, Maine, to walk along the cliff path and rock outcroppings. As we hike along the edge, listening to the roar of the waves, the sun is blotted out by a bank of black clouds. We seek shelter in the Ship's Cellar Pub at York Harbor Inn. Its wood-paneled walls are done up in the manner of an old wooden schooner. Its windows are rounded portholes, its ceilings and walls bend in and curve like a boat. We sit in its forepeak next to a wood-burning fire throwing a faint scent of earth into the room as a rain storm rages outside.

The earth surrounding my shed is sprouting little green ears. They are Canadian mayflowers, and they are coming up everywhere, as if the earth is listening to itself exhale and groan its way into yet another springtime through these tiny, delicate membranes. During an evening's waning light, Frank uses a manual post-hole digger to break up the earth to the left of my studio and we plant another small shade garden, which I am hoping will reinvigorate the yard to some extent. We transplant plume flowers, white pearls, superbells, and windflowers, and, of course, ferns that are guaranteed to thrive anywhere. Hopefully, the deer will overlook my small garden for feasts elsewhere.

It's twilight on a soft spring day, and I step up into my writing shed to light the white pillar candle inside its glass chimney. Frank has helped me hang three wooden shelves along the back wall: Two—one above the other—on the left, and one on the right. I admire their symmetry. Outside in the ravine, the forest is a luminous green as the last vestige of light rises up to meet and mingle with the coming dark.

I continue researching how to build a string of three steps up into the shed. Another trip to the mega home improvement store yields little help with this particular project. Not one sales associate we asked knew a thing about step construction. On returning home, I check out YouTube for wisdom on the subject. It all starts to seem too much for the day. I walk back to the shed to give it the bad news that step construction is on hold. A painted turtle that had worked its way up the ravine while we were gone "runs" loops around the back yard as it investigates its new turf. It appears to have more energy than I do at the moment. It moves swiftly for a turtle, stopping every once in a while to crane its yellow-and-green-striped neck up over tufts of low-lying grass. Instead of hammering away at stair risers, I watch the turtle do a full "360" around the yard before thrusting itself back over the edge of the ravine, where it tumbles into undergrowth.

Something somewhere suddenly has happened. I only catch the last snippet of news as I turn into our long, gravel drive. My cellphone rings as I pull up to the garage with a trunk full of groceries. "I'm all right," Bethany assures me. "I'm fine." But I don't know why she might not be "fine" until she tells me: There has been an explosion at the finish line of the Boston Marathon. The water station where she was posted as a volunteer was a full five miles away—nowhere near the carnage. She says she is fine, and I must believe this to be true, but who is really fine in light of this? I am distraught and distressed and disturbed, not to mention anguished by the fact that something of this magnitude has occurred so close to home and caused so much suffering. My family may have been spared personal fallout from this disastrous event, but other families have not.

As I ring off from Bethany, I feel the need to find a place of connection, where I can reorient myself in the world. Curiously, I do not make my way to a church or other official house of worship as I did on 9/11, when I joined others at a spontaneous interfaith service at the Congregational Church in town. The new me coming to the fore suddenly wants silence, and the solace of nature. I can't retreat to my shed. It's still a construction zone and reeks of stain, so I go to the only other place I know where I can be alone and cocooned in nature. I take myself to the Audubon sanctuary at the end of our street and walk along the river trail, hoping I'll see the chickadees. I come upon them near the pond's boardwalk. They are hopping and pecking about on the forest floor and flitting about in massive gnarled vines above. I stand among them, still and silent, and let them minister to me. First one alighted on my hand, its little trident feet gripping the tip of my forefinger. And then another and another. Three little chickadees came to be with me as I asked for benediction for the world and drew a mantle of healing and care around those in pain, in shock, and lost to the destruction of the blast.

I arrive home from the Audubon sanctuary to find a yellow female warbler sitting strangely on our back deck. I open the sliding door and crouch down beside her to ask what is wrong. She fearlessly returns my gaze. All the questions and answers of the universe are contained in her liquid, little black eyes. Within seconds, she turns her head to the side and tucks it under her wing. I can see she is on her way into another world. I lean in closer to tell her how precious she is, how this world has loved having her in it. I tell her how beautiful her soft yellow plumage is. And then, just as I finish singing her praises, her little body goes limp. She flops over, her spindly stick-like legs suddenly thrust out behind her. I pick her up and carry her to the edge of the woods, where I lay her to rest in a bed of pachysandra. "Good night, sweetheart," I say, unable to make any sense of the day.

Chapter 7

Conversations with Mother Earth

It is the yellow season. Daffodils are giving way to forsythia—little tufts of yellow fingers bursting forth from what appears to be dried, dead sticks. Suddenly, I'm awash in memory. My child self steps to the fore.

"I saw you dancing in the forsythia bushes the other day," said our elderly neighbor Miss Glidden, who had just come from the funeral of her even more elderly mother and was at our house for dinner at the behest of my mother. I—all of 10 years old—blushed furiously.

"You did?" was all I could think to say.

"Yes," she said, fingering her short strand of pearls with her humped, arthritic knuckles. "I did. I was wondering if you were pretending to be at a coming-out ball, or a cotillion?" I knew Miss Glidden lived in a different universe than my big, rambunctious family but I didn't know just how foreign it was until she started telling tales of 'coming out' as a debutante in the early 1900s. At the time, I didn't know what a debutante or a cotillion was, but I was savvy enough to listen to an old woman reminisce on the night she had buried her mother—her last remaining relative. I wasn't about to tell her that I had pulled on the long, full-skirted yellow dress from our dress-up collection—a motley assortment of cast-off clothes from my mother's closet that we kept in a chest on the side porch— because it was the exact color of the forsythia flowers in bloom along our driveway. I had gone to stand beneath the brittle arches of the bush as a nod to our shared yellowness. I hadn't meant to dance at all while I was under there, but then I started twirling the long yellow skirts out around me like a flowering bud, and I could not stop. I was one with the forsythia flowers. In fact, I wanted to *be* a forsythia flower. The forsythia bush had been my portal to ecstatic experience. I had experienced eternity among the flowers. At the time, I never would have been able to identify the experience in quite this way. All I knew then was that I had lost track of time inside a capsule of supreme happiness. I wasn't about to share any of this with Miss Glidden, who had witnessed what I thought was my private moment of connection and enchantment.

The saga of the steps continues. I decide to call in reinforcements, which means that Frank has agreed to accompany me on yet another trip to the mega home improvement warehouse. Some salesmen, I have noticed during this lengthy shed construction enterprise, have taken me less than seriously when I have asked for help purchasing building materials. Some ignored or overlooked me when I was clearly overwhelmed and wandering down the aisles in search of something or other. Some have over-explained simple construction concepts. And a few haven't bothered to explain at all what would have made a particular task go smoother. In any event, Frank has agreed to accompany me because I am now at a loss as to how to start stair construction and I need him to be a good interrogator and listener once we lasso a salesman who knows a thing or two about stair construction. Alas, not one employee we initially spoke with could help. "Steps?" One asked with a blank expression. No. He was sorry. He was without a clue how to begin, didn't even know where step-construction supplies were stored inside the store. He eventually worked up the muster to show us metal joists that even to Frank's and my untrained eyes didn't look sturdy enough to secure three wooden steps to the base of a shed. There we stood, surrounded on all sides by towering shelves of boards, wooden posts and pre-cut wooden moldings, all suggesting that sturdy stairs could be constructed from their rough and grainy forms, if only someone could tell us how and help us buy the supplies we needed. We decided it was time to take our business to the other mega home improvement warehouse only a few miles away. That's where fate smiled on us in the form of a young sales associate named Kyle. "What you need are 'stringers,'" he said.

Sensing a sympathetic soul, I sketched out the entire project for Kyle in living color: The rescued Andersen windows, the walls Marilyn and I insulated, the birds that have come to call. I tell him about the shed's location at the edge of a ravine, that it had been christened at the factory as just another 'Country Carriage' but that I have taken to calling it The Bird's Nest. Kyle listened attentively, which I appreciated even more than his efficient know-how. When I was done, he got back to being all business. "Like I said, you need three 'stringers.' They will support the steps. You can't just get one for each end of the steps. You'll want one in the middle, too. "

That's when he placed bright-orange traffic cones at each end of an aisle, hopped in the seat of a great beeping conveyance with flashing lights, and used its controls to raise two steel arms up into the nether reaches of warehouse shelving to retrieve a shrink-wrapped pad of pre-cut wooden step stringers. Then he cut the steps' backing boards to the proper measurement, located properly-sized stair treads, and ran up and down aisles collecting all the appropriate hardware I would need to assemble my shed's steps. I wished I could bring him home.

I am so excited about the possibility of building the steps that I wake up in the middle of the night. They are the last major construction component of the entire shed and I feel reasonably sure that—with Frank's help and a power tool or two—I can get them made and affixed to the shed just beneath its doorframe. I see my way forward! What a difference a day makes. My little house, my studio, my Bird's Nest, will soon be anchored to the earth. It will no longer be levitating on cement blocks, no longer appear to be unmoored. I rouse myself from bed to look out the back window at my shed—a barely visible rectangular shadow among the trees. All is dark. All is still. All is silent. The animals are sleeping and dreaming animal dreams. I picture myself ascending three small, sturdy steps instead of grabbing onto the shed's door frame and hoisting myself awkwardly across the threshold. I am amazed at what focus and patience can accomplish. That I have made all of this take shape in the universe seems a miracle.

At three a.m., I am roused from sleep by honking geese winging by the house. How are they navigating air currents in the dark? The next morning, during a bike ride along the Ipswich River, I see a flotilla of them riding the river's current in tight geese formation. There's a leader, with an array of others fanned out behind it in a neat and tidy "V". Suddenly, the leader begins to trumpet, and takes off with a great beating of wings. One minute, it's floating on the water's surface and the next it's suspended in mid-air. Talk about accomplishment! Talk about a miracle.

The steps are completed. Finished! Done. In the end, it only takes Frank and me an afternoon to construct these tidy transitional platforms up and into the shed. After I lay the last coat of mushroom-colored stain on the bottom tread, I stand back to admire our handiwork. The stain dries quickly, but not quickly enough for the chipmunks, squirrels, and robins hopping about the edge of the ravine. They are impatient to stake their claim. When I go out to the shed in the evening, I notice tiny paw prints silhouetted in the stain and half nibbled acorns scattered across the bottom stair tread. In building the steps, I hadn't realized that I was also creating perfect picnic tables for small forest creatures.

Clucking, chirping, whistling, trilling, croaking, pecking, yammering. As spring continues to unfold into summer, Frank and I wake up to a cacophony. But the avian concert outside our bedroom window is nothing compared to the frenzied bird energy at the boatyard where The Flying Dutchman winters over. It's Memorial Day, which means only one thing to New England yachters: Get the boat in the water and be quick about it! Summers aren't nearly long enough. Every minute counts. The bird families that have made nests inside engine exhaust pipes and downed masts resting along the tops of cabins and cockpits are wild with activity. They have only just taught their chicks to fly. The fiberglass hulls and wooden ketches have been their home for the last several weeks, ports in storms so to speak, and now the nests are being ripped asunder and tossed among the marsh grasses by boaters crazed to get their vessels righted and back out on the water. Red-winged black birds, starlings, chickadees, robins—all are swooping about and trilling, calling out to one another in warning when yet another behemoth is yanked away from its parking place on land and backed into the launching area.

If we have past lives, in at least one Frank was a sea captain. In this life, he stops the car at every marina and harbor along the New England coast, often going miles and minutes out of his way in order to ogle a boat's lines. He lavishes care and attention on his own sailboat—a Sabre 28—every spring, polishing its hull, re-varnishing its wooden grab rails, "eyebrows," and other wooden accents around the cockpit, de-molding its interior, pumping out the engine's anti-freeze, and flushing its water lines. Having never taken dust cloth to cabinetry in the house, Frank painstakingly applies cleaning agents to toothbrush bristles in order to polish every corner and crevice of the Sabre's cabin and cockpit.

After weeks of varnishing and cleaning and preparing The Flying Dutchman for spring launch, Frank and Tyler climb a ladder up to the Sabre's cockpit to take command of the vessel. Fred, the owner and manager of the boatyard, positions his enormous trailer in front of the Sabre's supporting stands. An assistant pulls out the stands one by one as the hull comes to rest on padded supports while its 2,000-pound keel nestles tidily inside the trailer's bed. There's an expertise to boat hauling that a landlubber can't imagine, especially by an old-fashioned tidal boatyard that operates without benefit of more advanced scaffolding and pulley systems prevalent at bigger boatyards. At Fred's boatyard, it's a case of backing the trailer cradling the boat into the water, positioning the truck that's hauling the trailer that's supporting the boat at just the right place at the edge of the ramp, reeling out the exact length of reinforced steel cable to float the boat off the trailer while keeping it tethered, then releasing the boat to float without restraint. It's comical to see Frank and Tyler bouncing along the land in the Sabre's cockpit as the boat is hauled to the launch ramp. A boat that feels like a toy on ocean swells is an ocean liner on *terra firma*. I wave good-bye to Frank and Tyler after Fred has successfully deposited The Flying Dutchmen into the drink and watch them motor off on the watery path between swaying marsh grasses and swooping red-winged blackbirds. At low tide, this is nothing but mud and marsh, but at high tide it becomes another world. No wonder the birds are darting and calling all around us. Their homes are sailing out to sea. It is an overcast, chilled gray day—not the best for sailing around Cape Ann and into Beverly Harbor where The Flying Dutchman is moored for the summer. I watch the stealth of fog float in across the marshes, and shiver. I am glad to be a landlubber today.

Tyler is almost as enchanted with boats as Frank, and spent several months after high school working aboard a 100-foot wooden schooner called The Mystic Whaler. The first time I stepped aboard, I was taken aback, spooked even, by what can only be called the boat's presence. That I could feel its living, pulsating essence shocked me to no end. I have never remotely considered myself a sailor, though I've spent hours, days—weeks—on the water with Frank. But, I suddenly realize, a wooden boat communicates in ways that fiberglass or steel ones do not.

"Did you feel that?" I asked Tyler when I followed him to his cabin below decks. "Can you hear the boat?"

"Of course," he said. "We talk at night. I call her The Mighty Mystic—after the Reggae song."

I want to know what they talk about, what The Mighty Mystic has to say as "she" plows through the waves, but I do not pry. The vessel oozes a sense of mystery and mysticism—a touchstone for some unseen reality. I think it has been aptly named, though Tyler tells me its name only references its port of origin in Mystic, Connecticut, that there's nothing all that mystical about it. When Frank was Tyler's age, he asked a palm reader, who for some reason happened to be hosting a booth at a boat show, if she "saw the sea" in his hands. If nothing else, the Sperry Topsiders Frank was wearing would have clued her in. The fact that he was attending a boat show would have clinched it. We laughed about it afterwards, but Frank was serious. If he would allow himself to be hypnotized, he would recall originating from the briny deep. He would remember emerging whole from gardens of seaweed, crawling ashore, shrugging off his crustacean shell, and learning how to stand. Frank was not born on a boat, but, I am told, he was conceived on one. This might explain his propensity for all things that float. It might also explain his uncanny sensitivity to wind modulations. Like Mary Poppins, he can step out our front door and size up the direction and strength of the wind. "It's a beam's reach to the Isles of Shoals today," he will sing-song after retrieving the newspaper at the end of our gravel drive and sniffing the wind. He pictures the day's most advantageous point of sail as he sips his morning coffee and reads the headlines.

On the boat, Frank is always right. I repeat: Frank is always right whenever we are on the boat. It is the one place I do whatever he says without equivocation. I am a guest in his world, a welcome interloper who makes sandwiches, serves drinks, descends into the cabin in a sudden squall to tighten up the hatches. Nonetheless, I'm an interloper. Frank is in charge, which, on a beautiful sunny day off the coast of Rockport's Thacher Island, saves us. I am half dozing in the sun when I notice he has perked his head up on high alert. "Let loose the genoa—now!" he barks. "Pull down the main!" He is feverishly loosening lines and ducking for cover from a sudden swing of the boom. I can't imagine what the problem is. I scamper up and scan the placid horizon for rocks as Frank stands tight-fisted at the helm. I yank down the sails. And then it hits—gust after gust. A squall pitches The Flying Dutchman sideways, sending me sprawling in the cockpit and dishes flying around galley cabinets below. Like rogue waves, rogue winds can rush in out of nowhere. Only sailors who have the sea in their hands can hear the coming assault.

Work on a boat is never done, even after it has been put in the water for the summer. While Frank works on The Flying Dutchman's electrical wiring during Memorial Day weekend, I stay home to paint patio furniture, pot plants, and head north as well as south for some adventuring. In either direction there is a bank of fog stubbornly sitting at the lip of the land around Massachusetts Bay. On Saturday afternoon, Bethany and I head up and over the Annisquam Bridge toward Gloucester and Rockport. The sun that had been brilliant all day at our house dulls into a gray sheen. By the time we arrive in Rockport, an encroaching fog has gathered into an enormous gray bank pillowing the tiny T-shirt shops on Bearskin Neck and stone jetty off Rockport's Dock Square. The rounded white steeple of the Congregational Church, where bagpipers play on New Year's Eve, slices gray skies. Its bell tolls through thick air. Tourists run into souvenir shops to buy flannel sweatshirts instead of T-shirts. Bethany stops for an ice cream cone. She is determined to celebrate the beginning of summer the way she always does. She can eat ice cream in any weather—even wearing a down parka and gloves. I, however, cannot, and duck into a shop for a fix of Earl Grey tea. Unlike the tourists "from away," she and I have come prepared with jackets. "You could get frostbite out there!" we overhear a man with a tanning-bed complexion complain. Bethany and I exchange glances: *Clearly, he is not from around these parts.*

Azaleas bloom around the same time as lilacs—perhaps just a little before—and just as their lovely jewel-tone pinks and fuchsias and magentas are giving way to muddy brown decay, it is the season of inchworms. The tiny trapeze artists swirl and sway at the end of invisible threads hanging from gutters and tree branches. Next come the enormous rhododendron bushes that line our front walk. What a dramatic and grand visual feast they are! Such exquisite balls of beauty from such tough, fibrous buds. I register these changes in our yard the way Frank reads the wind.

Finally! The interior of my shed is stained and polished to a sheen! I am as obsessed about its appearance and maintenance as Frank is about The Flying Dutchman. From around the house, I assemble notepads, pens, blank journals, art supplies, books about writing, and a few other accessories and transport everything out to my shed. The tufted-wool cardinal pillow Frank's mother made me years ago is the perfect accessory for my shed's visitor chair. An entire year has now passed since I began keeping a journal about building my shed. I only have a few last-minute construction touches and then I'll be done, but it's finished enough now that I can begin to bask inside its honey-oak interior as I compose poems, short "snapshot essays," and journals at my mother's antique writing desk, which Frank and I carried gingerly out to my shed and centered beneath the two Andersen windows overlooking the ravine.

In order to furnish the large, high-ceilinged rooms of the drafty Victorian my father bought for our growing family in 1959, my mother frequented a junk/antique shop called the Dover Store. Once a month, my father would drive her out to Dover on a Saturday afternoon to see what unsung treasures she could find among the piles of bric-a-brac and dusty, decrepit furniture. I can only assume her writing desk originated in that place, though I can't recall her triumphant return with it strapped to the roof of our station wagon. Her refinishing and re-upholstering skills were on par with any professional, which allowed her to transform hideous, junky finds into lovely showcase pieces. Only she could see the merit in a scratched up old table top or filthy winged-back upholstered chair. The rest of us were always blind to the hidden charms and merits of the junk she brought home until she re-worked them and displayed them in all their new-found glory. Her antique writing desk was no different. After she had refinished it, it occupied a place of honor at the base of our front hall's grand wooden staircase. But after more than 50 years, the desk is looking a little worn. I glue the desk's rotting joints so that it doesn't teeter and threaten to collapse when I lean on it. Although its writing surface is just as substantial and lovely as it's ever been following my mother's ministrations, its undercarriage is a little wobbly. A block of wood fell off one of its gently-curving legs during its transportation from house to shed across our back clearing. I glue it all back together and keep the joint in place by tying a thick strip of white cloth around it while it dries, which makes it look as though the desk has a tooth ache. The cloth comes off soon enough, and I am pleased to see that my efforts have made the entire desk sturdier. It has occurred to me of late that it may be a come-down for my mother's desk to hold center stage inside my pre-fab shed when it once sat nobly beneath a stained-glass Victorian window in our expansive front hall. I figure that, as long as it is fulfilling its destiny as a writing desk, it must approve of its new location. I place a woven mat decorated with a singing chickadee on its surface and arrange my writing implements and notebooks in its drawers.

As a final nod to the natural artistry of my shed, I arrange rocks, sea shells, jars of sea glass, my feather collection, and small pieces of Marilyn's pottery along the rough-hewn shelving and wooden window sills. I look around admiringly and realize that the gift is this: I can be whomever I want inside these four walls. My writing studio is outfitted for dreams, stories, revelation, and reflection. I shall break the boundaries of everyday existence and see what unfolds! I decide to hold off smudging the interior of my shed with mountain sage and cedar sweet grass until Tyler has a chance to do it with me. He gave me a sacred smudging stick at Christmas, so that I may hold a Native American ceremony, asking for clarity and vision and healing and good intentions as my spirit and the spirit of my new small writing house at the edge of the ravine join forces. In sending forth aromatic herbs into its interior, I am dispelling any negative energy that may be lingering in its joists and boards. My inner critic definitely won't enter my shed after this. But apparently small forest creatures can. Way up on one of the ceiling trusses, I find mouse droppings and a partially nibbled nut. This does not set well with me. I may want to observe forest creatures from my "blind," but they are not invited inside to observe me. I will have to plug up some cracks along the roofline and spray foam insulation between the windows. I cannot provide shelter to any and all small creatures, as much as they may like it. On a trip to the Audubon sanctuary's visitor center, I happen upon a display that sheds light on my mouse visitor. White-footed mice are woodland dwellers that live in stumps, logs, and brush piles (plenty of all that surrounding my shed), and they are adept at climbing. Apparently, skittering along foundation stones and scaling the exterior paneling of my Bird's Nest is child's play for a white-footed mouse.

Exactly a year ago, the crab apple tree—the one I so carefully honored and integrated into the placement of my studio shed—was in full pale-pink majesty. But this year, there's nothing. Not a hint or hue of pink. It's just leaves. Does it bloom every year? I honestly don't know. Before the new me stepped in, I never bothered to notice how frequently the crab apple flowered. I hope I haven't disturbed its rhythms by locating my shed beneath its branches. I head over to a local nursery, where I'm hit with bad news.

"You traumatized your tree by excavating around it," the tree and shrub expert says. "Its roots couldn't draw necessary nutrients up to its branches. You're lucky it leafed out."

Oh! What was I thinking by disturbing the soil around its base?! I buy the bag of plant food he recommends and distribute it into the soil surrounding the trunk. I am hoping the delicate little tree will recover, that it will forgive me. There are so many apologies to be made in life. I tell the crab apple how sorry I am that I have interfered with her intent to blossom. As I spread the plant food around the tree, I notice more jacks-in-the-pulpit springing up around the area. Even though I thought I had transplanted all of them from there last year, some have remained. They love growing in the shadows. Several poke their necks up from the pachysandra so they can get a good look around. There's nothing to do now but wait. I hope Miss Crab Apple can develop a new lease on life with the help of all this nitrogen, phosphate, soluble potash calcium, and other assorted ingredients contained in the organic plant food. All I can contribute to the situation now is patience.

Another concern has gathered in the back of my mind: The frogs and toads in the ravine's vernal pond seem to be quieter this year. I wonder what the problem is, or if there is a problem at all. I hope they are not joining ranks with the threatened blue-spotted salamander. Usually at twilight, the raucous calypso is ear-splitting. I am hoping my concern for our amphibian neighbors is unfounded, that humans haven't interfered with their numbers, that I haven't affected their existence in the vernal pond below. Perhaps it's just a normal, natural causation? I simply don't know. But if the ravine doesn't sound like the Amazonian jungle this year, it sure looks like it. The enormous fern fronds are out, jubilantly and riotously doing back bends in circles as the sun slants through an opening in the leaf canopy. I am concerned that the construction of my shed has interrupted the habits of deer, many of whom traverse a trail from the ravine and up along the back of the ridge to nearby Averill Street. The number of deer ambling through our yard seems to be diminishing since I have constructed my shed. I have imposed myself upon the land, and in doing so, I'm sure I have altered the patterns of this place. There's no help for it now. I'm hoping the animals and plants learn to take my presence and alterations in stride.

Like it or not, little ground creatures seek safety under my shed as a matter of course. At first, it was bunnies. Then it was squirrels and chipmunks. Now a groundhog seems to be the queen of the castle. I watch it make its way across the back yard clearing and assume it's the same one that appeared the morning after I surrendered to my middle-aged self in a dream. It stops to investigate something at the base of a mayapple and then moves on. It's a bold, little creature, though it glances around furtively to see if anyone might be watching. I look up information about groundhogs again in my New England field guide, and find that it is also known as a woodchuck, land beaver, or (my favorite) whistle-pig. Basically, it's just a large ground squirrel. I name it "Sparky" because I don't know its gender and this seems to be a gender-neutral name. Plus, at this point, I feel it needs a name. It has been visiting me on and off ever since I started thinking about building my shed. I call Jane, my animal totem expert, to tell her the groundhog is back. She is not surprised.

Is there anything more poetic than the arms of a lilac bush waving and calling for attention over the top of a New England stone wall in the rain? The lilacs at their peak are arching and bending, nearly drowning in the rain, their pale-purple throats running with rivulets of water. The tiny peepers in the vernal pond love this weather. They sing and sing all evening, which reassures me greatly. They are overjoyed with the wet! But I can't plant, and neither can I paint. I have cans of Naples Blue and Viking Yellow near the back door, just waiting to give a new lease on life to tired, old patio furniture. I have pots of ground cover and lavender and lemon balm waiting to go into the ground and porch pots. But all is on hold. Instead of painting or planting on my afternoon off work, I head the 10 minutes up to Marini Farm. I am in search of fresh asparagus. I buy the last three bunches for almost $10. It seems an astronomical price until I am biting into a purple-green stalk garnished with a hint of lemon juice and freshly ground pepper. We may be laboring under a deluge, but all is right in the universe if the ground can unfurl such gustatory magnificence.

During a recent visit to the Audubon sanctuary, I learn how to cook a mean dandelion stir-fry. (Who knew dandelions mix well with red bell peppers?) The recipe calls for the heads of fresh, young dandelions picked first thing in the morning, when dew adds a hint of flavor. Once the heads are washed and dipped in egg and flour, they must be tossed into a well-oiled skillet with herbs and peppers (or any other vegetable of choice) for browning. The recipe suggests serving this versatile side dish along with Boston baked beans and barbeque chicken. I learn that fiddlehead ferns can substitute for dandelion heads, should one's lawn be miraculously void of dandelions, but I am hard-pressed to say that ferns taste like anything at all. Frank refuses to eat dandelions or ferns—or anything else, for that matter, that resembles what he calls "rabbit food."

One cool overcast evening, Frank announces that The Flying Dutchman's engine is not working properly. He has to sail the boat to a marina upriver from the yacht club for repairs. Wonderful memories of sailing up Newbury's Parker River 25 years ago in Frank's Corinthian 19 whisper to me that I should go along. Just before sunset, we let loose from the mooring for a magical trip up river and under the Salem-Beverly Bridge. It's a voyage of great egrets fishing along the river's edge next to basking turtles and overhanging willows. There are houses with private docks where owners sit—drinks in hand—to witness the sun's glide into low-lying clouds. It's also a voyage of engineering genius. Frank tunes the boat's two-way radio to channel 13 in order to contact keepers of bridges that bar our passage at various intervals. Bridge-keepers crank up sirens, switch on flashing yellow-and-red warning lights, and lower guardrails so that bridges swing open to allow the passage of The Flying Dutchman and its crew of two. All coming and going of street traffic stops to allow us to make way. We are the only sailing vessel out at this time of twilight. There are a few motor boats as well as various lone fishermen on docks and jetties silently watching our progress from shore. A cormorant riding a bobbing mooring ball spreads its wings to dry in the breeze and pays homage to the dying of the day. With the wind propelling us from behind, Frank lets the mainsail out on one side of the boat and the jib on the other so that we are sailing 'wing-and-wing.' As Frank navigates the narrow chan- nel along a curving watery path, I am lost in serenity, wishing I had watercolors and notebook in hand. I glance over to see Frank's furrowed brow. He is worried about the engine, I know.

I elect not to join a community supported agriculture program. Doing so would tie me into going to the same farm stand every week and require that I give over hundreds of dollars up front. Instead, I scope out which stand has the best prices and best produce each week. Marini Farm is high on my list for corn-on-the-cob and asparagus. It's also where I pick strawberries in late June. I go to Russell Orchards, located on the way to Crane Beach, to pick blueberries, apples, and pumpkins. And, just before Thanksgiving, I go to Russell's in search of golden seckle pears, miniature versions of larger pear cousins, to jumble in among apples and clementines in my holiday fruit bowl. At one of my farm stand haunts, I learn that nasturtiums and johnny-jump-ups are considered "salad flowers." I am surprised to see their little faces peeking out of Ziploc sandwich bags. Apparently, the colorful little garden flowers are the perfect garnish. Their yellow, orange, and cornflower-blue petals are sup-posed to make a world of difference in a salad's presentation, their combined peppery, minty flavor pleasing to the palate. I think they are too beautiful to eat and leave them for others to sprinkle among cucumbers and carrots.

The joy of pick-your-own fruits and berries at farm stands is to be immersed in the tastes and flavors and feel of the motion, though most proprietors frown on eating while picking. But this is a lot to ask. If you can't savor the flavor of fruit fresh from the stem, why not save yourself from the scald of the sun and the bite of the bugs? Why not just stand at the cash register and pay for pints of berries picked by other hands? I am drawn to the slant of the afternoon sun, the breezes, the stroll down a dirt road that takes me past peach trees and apple orchards to the berry patch. I want to be out among the crickets, the far-off hum of a tractor engine, roosters crowing in the distance, and songbirds whistling in the wind. I'm convinced that all of it—the entire experience and effort of it—makes my blueberry cobblers and apple pies taste so much better. Nothing about the experience feels the least bit "chore-like."

Long Hill, the mansion once home to famed *Atlantic Monthly* editor Ellery Sedgwick, is the only place I know where the public is invited to pick flowers. Bachelor's buttons, zinnias, calendula, sunflowers, dahlias, snapdragons, and scabiosa—each row is segmented one from the other and identified with a colorful, hand-painted sign created by staff of the Trustees of Reservations, which now owns and operates the historic property in Beverly. The price for the pleasure of wandering up and down rows of swirling, scented flower fields and snipping away? Eight dollars for 20 stems. I revel in an orgy of color before handing the volunteer $20 and heading home to trim stalks and arrange flowers in small vases placed on bedroom dressers, at the lip of bathroom sinks, in the middle of the kitchen island. I stoop to breathe in the scent and admire the symmetrical arrangement of petals as I putter from room to room.

The jacks-in-the-pulpit I transplanted last year have forgiven me! Their strange hooded heads are unfurling in the woodland garden I created at the edge of our back clearing. When I moved them from the base of the crab apple, I thought for sure I had destroyed their group dynamics and upset their equilibrium. But, no.

They have returned, just as I asked them to. The two most mature plants are very different from each other. One has a plum-colored "tongue" and wildly striped hood of deep purple and green reminiscent of a beach umbrella or circus tent. The other is albino— white and ivory all around.

On a quick day-trip to the coast of Maine, Frank and I stop at St. Anthony's Franciscan Monastery, where we discover the grounds' wooded path edged by small, triangular-roofed twig niches attached to trees. Inside the niches are statues of saints. I decide I must assemble my own small, twigged niches on trees edging my shade garden. What I shall place inside them is not yet apparent. Most likely, I will decorate them with acorns or pinecones or images of dragonflies, birds, or dandelions—ordinary elements of creation that barely get noticed at all.

Tasks still to be completed on my shed:

- Affix homemade clay tiles above interior door jam;
- Lay slate stones for pathway and garden area;
- Write out Bethany's poetry on wooden panel; affix above front window.

As soon as I tell my hairdresser about my garden and shed project, she invites me to help myself to the spread of lilies-of-the-valley in her back yard. "Take as many as you like," she says. "They're taking over my entire garden." I drive over with trowel and shovel, along with the large plastic lids of our garbage pails to use as trays. I scoop out the little, white-headed flowers along with tiny pale-purple violets woven in among their roots and transport the ground cover to my woodland garden. I tuck them into bed among the mayapples, ajuga, and jacks-in-the-pulpit. An old musical round surfaces in my mind—a memory of Mrs. Kilroy's fourth-grade class:

> *White choral bells upon a slender stalk,*
> *Lilies of the valley deck my garden walk.*
> *Oh don't you wish that you could hear them ring?*
> *That will happen only when the fairies sing.*

There is no one to chime in at just the right place to make the weaving harmonics of the round. I am a soloist singing to the plants, extending as much encouragement and good will as I can in their direction.

In truth, I speak to flowers and animals and plants and trees on a regular basis. I did not realize this is a natural and normal response to the land until I stumbled upon Canadian artist Rebecca Belmore's "Megaphone Project" at a museum in Vancouver, Canada. I stood transfixed inside a small exhibit hall as I listened to recordings of people from all walks of life address Mother Earth through an oversized megaphone that Belmore had toted from place to place and set up in public squares. *"What would you like to say to the earth?"* She had asked strangers who unabashedly approached her. Many indigenous people chanted in their native tongue, others prayed and recited poems or read reflections aloud. All expressed their love outright in tender reverence. Many also expressed regret for humans' disrespect and carelessness of the earth. Their voices— so sincere and full of longing, love, and apology—brought tears to my eyes. I wondered what I would say into Rebecca's oversized megaphone, were she to travel to Topsfield. What would I broadcast to the forests and wetlands of the ravine? To the Ipswich and Essex Rivers? To Crane Beach and surrounding marshlands? What could I possibly say?

A blast furnace of a weekend has descended on Boston's North Shore. Frank and I get up early to decide on a plan of action, which includes washing and re-staining the back deck before the midday sun sky-rockets the thermometer to 120 degrees in full sun. We then head to Crane Beach, where we loll around in the surf along with everyone else in search of relief. We go back later for an evening swim before making our way to The Flying Dutchman waiting for us on its mooring in Beverly Harbor. A strong, hot wind blows and blows all night long. It blows right down the front hatch of the boat, where Frank and I lay cradled inside the forepeak, not so much sleeping as stunned into oblivion by the heat of the day, the gentle lap-lap of waves against the hull, and the boat's hypnotic rocking. On Sunday, we awake before dawn to debilitating heat once again. We decide to abandon ship. We stop for breakfast at the Depot Diner in Beverly and then head for home, grab our bikes, and pedal up to Hood Pond before it opens. We skirt around the locked gate and down to the docks, where we peel down to our "skivvies" and cannon-ball off the dock. There is no point in staying home in such heat. We know our one anemic air conditioner will deliver only slightly cooled air and that we will feel imprisoned in the house. Instead, we head up north to Wolfeboro, New Hampshire, for a wild, wet loop around Lake Winnipesaukee in the rumble seat of a rented vintage power boat.

Later that week, when friends Kate and Ron visit from Colorado, Kate wants some suggestions for sight-seeing with us. "There's Newport, Rhode Island," I tell her, "with its mansions and harbor full of million-dollar yachts. Or there's Penobscot Bay in Maine, where we could sail aboard a windjammer and eat seafood on a restaurant pier. Or what about Franconia Notch in the White Mountains of New Hampshire? We could go hiking." Kate is understandably flummoxed by the choices, not to mention the number of states, I have uttered in one breath. "Is all that doable? I thought we were visiting you in Massachusetts," she says. But that's the way of it. You can get from Boston's North Shore to another state in a matter of minutes or a couple of hours—a completely foreign concept in the Midwest where it used to take us seven hours just to drive across the great state of Kansas and still not be anywhere of interest. During our time there, we spent many weekends at my behest in search of wagon ruts, swales cut into the wide, western prairies by pioneer wagons traversing the Oregon Trail 150 years earlier. I was intrigued when older Kansans I met told me that the wagon ruts were still clearly visible when they were children in the 1960s. I took us to every possible wagon rut sighting and museum and monument dedicated to the pioneers I could find. If Frank was a sea captain in a former life, I believe I must have been a pioneer in mine. Otherwise, my infatuation with the prairies and pioneers is entirely inexplicable.

After considering the array of sight-seeing choices in New England, Kate decides we should take the ferry to Martha's Vineyard, where life proves never to be a replay of itself. The last time Frank and I cycled along the Shining Sea Bike Path from Falmouth to Woods Hole and hopped the ferry to Martha's Vineyard we biked in baking heat. This time, with Kate and Ron as our companions, the soaring steel beams of the Bourne Bridge cut upwards into a layer of dank fog. The car's thermometer drops from 86 to 73 degrees as we cross the Cape Cod Canal. Have jackets will travel. Ours, of course, are in the trunk. In the meantime, we shut down the air conditioning and crank up the heat. We decide to park at the ferry terminal and rent bikes on the island. The National Security Alert is at yellow, which, according to the sign posted inside the Woods Hole Steamship Authority Terminal, means "elevated." I'm not sure how this affects our ferry-crossing, except that there are signs instructing passengers to refrain from using cellphones while boarding. Once in Oak Bluffs on 'the Vineyard,' we are again in brilliant sunshine. Martha's Vineyard in the summer is a New England idyll. Every clapboard cottage—or mansion, for that matter—is stained the same pale blue-gray patina, compliments of perpetual sea spray. So many of the wood-shingled houses are surrounded by exquisite gardens of wisteria, wildflowers, lilacs, rhododendrons, and geraniums. And every house is edged with a porch or patio, where tubs of impatiens and phlox spill over low stone walls.

We locate a bike rental shop and take off on bikes toward a charming enclave of gingerbread cottages erected in the late 1800s as part of a religious camp community. The cottages are a crayon box of colors. Their delicate scrollwork, miniature front porches, curly cupolas and open–air sleeping porches are from another era. We exit the charming little community and head along the waterfront toward Edgartown. From Vineyard Haven to Oak Bluffs to Edgartown, people are biking, running, ambling, or playing Frisbee on front lawns that sweep around expansive porches encircled by rhododendrons and hydrangeas. Here, the fog has evaporated into thin air. Returning to the mainland the next day, the ferry is packed. We slam into fog as we are halfway across Vineyard Sound. It rises up from the ferry's deck like sheer panels of drapery fabric. Through the gauze of gray, the sun is a muted, translucent disc hanging in the sky.

Chapter 8
Forest Creep

Some days are easy to be alive. They require only a modicum of effort along with vats of iced tea and homemade potato salad consumed under the ceiling fan on the back porch. On this particular day, the temperature is mild. The sun is out, but not hot. I swing in and out of the back door on the faintest currents of air. I can't get enough of days like this; I can't make them last long enough. They are gifts from the summer gods. Only those who have lived in other parts of the country more desolate, more humid, more rainy, or otherwise more disagreeable can truly appreciate the crystal-cut sun of a New England summer day, when white clapboard houses and weathered barns appear to levitate on grassy inclines. Every summer we lived in the stultifying heat and humidity of Virginia and Kansas, Frank and I would bring the kids back to Boston's North Shore to visit family. The trip up the East Coast from Virginia under cover of darkness while Bethany and Tyler slept in the back of our VW camper van was the most dramatic of our returns. Somewhere in the vicinity of Stamford, Connecticut—long about two in the morning—Frank and I would turn off the air conditioning, lower the car windows, and exalt in the freshening air. "Do you smell that?" we would marvel. "New England! Oh, thank God!" By the time we rolled into my mother-in-law's driveway close to dawn, we were coveting a dip in her back yard pool, which was always a frosty 65 degrees. Pulling on fleeces and flannels—flannels!—afterwards was a particular joy. Goosebumps were gifts. Now, after years of being back in New England, we still thrill to the summer air.

I go shopping in downtown Ipswich on this lovely summer afternoon. The centuries-old Choate Bridge is festooned with flower boxes; its reflection is making a complete circle of itself in the river below. It's lovely. It's atmospheric. It's amazing that it has withstood floods and vehicular traffic of some sort since 1764. It is the oldest stone double-arched bridge in North America, and the town is commemorating its distinguished history with a parade. The Ipswich River curls through town past art galleries, offices, and condos housed in historic mills and first-period homes dating to the late 1600s and early 1700s. The town's much newer pedestrian bridge spans the river just below the dam and fish ladder. I stop into Zumis for a quick cappuccino and think I could be somewhere in Europe.

I conjure up France or Switzerland. That's how fresh the air is in this tiny, tidy river town on this stellar summer day.

On the way home, I pass by farm workers haying in fields that line Routes 133 and 1A as well as at the intersection of Ipswich Road and Asbury Street in Topsfield. Tractors are pulling baling machines through fields of long-stemmed cut grass. Some of the balers spit out the traditional rectangular small bales. Others deliver up enormous hay rounds that are positioned on their sides at various intervals across the fields. The large, spherical bales remind me of rural France, especially as the sun sinks into the horizon and gives way to the gloaming—another word from another time that I love. Gloaming is the precursor to twilight, when the sun lays a golden path across the land and shadows creep in along the edge.

On a stormy Friday night after work, we drive up to Maine in a downpour. Sheets of water slam the windshield, as if we are traveling inside an automatic car wash. We check into a modest motel just north of Camden after dark, and get soaked dashing from car to room. The next day, we awake to discover Penobscot Bay glistening and glinting in spectacular sunshine outside our window, which means a visit to the annual Maine Boats, Homes, and Harbors Show in Rockland is in order. Frank spends hours ambling about the boats in the harbor while I weave in and out of vendor booths showcasing decorative arts, ingenious kitchen gadgets, and gardening ideas. In Rockland Harbor, I watch two boys harvest bucketfuls of periwinkles that are the size of my thumbnail. Using nothing but their bare hands, the boys push away rubbery strands of seaweed to scrape crustaceans from slimy boulders. The tiny barnacles are supposed delicacies—miniature escargot. I cannot imagine having the patience to scoop flesh from shell. And for what? The taste of briny muscular tissue no larger than a dried pea? I prefer clam chowder. Chunks of potatoes. Thick cream. Onion. Parsley and black pepper garnish. That's an easy choice.

Why do pathways mowed through fields of waist-high wildflowers call my name? We stay two nights in the Strawberry Hill Seaside Inn in Rockport, Maine, where we discover just such a landscape leading down to the sea. It is pure enchantment. To walk sloping grass paths surrounded by a wild plumage of lavender, cornflower-blue, fuchsia, ivory, every hue of yellow imaginable, and pale-pink suggests secret worlds. As we meander down the paths to the Adirondack chairs facing the cove, we notice tiny, narrow entrances into the scrub of these flowering fields. Clearly, little ground creatures have made their own hidden pathways. We watch a red-tailed fox scoot along the edge of the meadow before disappearing into dense undergrowth. Tall grasses close in behind its tail, concealing its entrance.

After sunset, a full moon creates a shimmery path on the black waters of Clam Cove. The little ones—crickets, bees, dragon-flies, cicadas and all sorts of other insects—hum and whir and chirp all evening and into the night, singing us to sleep through the screen of our balcony door. Their low-level chorus is a constant no matter what time of day we are out and about on the pathways. They can't help themselves. They, along with a multitude of songbirds, are living in heaven among unmown fields of wildflowers. We spend the next day taking naps and reading beside the hotel's two pools, each surrounded by diminutive waterfalls, enormous spreads of goat's beard, miniature pines, and colorful pots of geraniums and impatiens. For our meals, we choose nearby modest restaurants overlooking the water that serve us blackened haddock on a bed of salad and homemade cream of broccoli soup followed by blueberry cheesecake, blueberry compote, blueberry pudding, or any other sweet folded through with the berries that grow along Maine's highways, fields, pastures, and barrens.

I am entranced by the sheep we see "baaing" and bleating in fields along our drives around the area. At Swans Island woolen headquarters in Northport, Maine, we discover that sheep are routinely transported to coastal islands to encourage the growth of extra thick fleece as protection in the harsh, exposed environment. This fleece, of course, results in superior wool for Swans Island weavers and spinners. In the woolen company's showroom, I discover its signature marketing image: A photo of a newly-shorn flock of sheep crossing the open sea in a longboat pulled by a commercial fishing vessel. The showroom is a stunning cascade of woolen goods. Blankets, shawls, throws, pillows, and scarves all clamor for attention. Draped across wooden racks staggered across wide pine floors, the display is arresting in its sparse artistry. As a splurge, Frank buys me an exquisite ivory-colored scarf woven with the company's distinctive insignia. I don't receive it until Christmas, as a surprise. It comes wrapped in a linen box accompanied by a little storybook about the cottage industry. The buttery soft scarf is certainly gift enough; the storybook—a beautifully-crafted marketing piece featuring the distinctive photo of sheep heading out to sea—is an unexpected bonus. When the scarf isn't draped across my shoulders, I store both it and the storybook in the linen box. It's only natural that I would thank the sheep for the wool off their backs as I toss my scarf—the exact color of their fleece—across my shoulders on chilly days.

The storied waters of Maine are primeval. Surf crashing into granite cliffs bears no resemblance to surf rolling into wide sandy beaches farther down the coast. Here, the water seems willful, a giant force to be reckoned with. Mariners who named these parts were poets. Eggemoggin Reach. Nubble Light. Pumpkin Knob. Their fanciful identifiers aptly convey the essential nature of this rocky region. Casco Bay's Pumpkin Knob could not be anything but a small island defined by an enormous hump of a boulder. As far as names go, it's perfect. I am also struck by the rivers that rush out to meet the sea along Maine's coast. There is so much energy in this collision of fresh and salt water. So much poetry. So much *currency*. Worlds collide at the mouths of rivers and sea. On our way home, we head south toward York Harbor, where we take one last meander along one of Maine's many coastal cliff walks. We don't get much exercise simply because we stop and sigh and admire and exclaim, postponing our departure from this glory land as long as possible. It is always a sinking feeling to leave the great heaving shoreline of Maine in our rearview mirror.

Dusk is wrapping its arms around our house. A soft rain has been falling for the past several hours, pattering against the mountain laurel outside the open dining room window. Gingerbread is baking in the oven, a bowl of freshly picked strawberries sits on the kitchen island. The rain has brought a presence to the evening silence. I am not alone—not really—even though no one else is here. The rain and the scent of gingerbread are keeping me company. I light beeswax candles on the screened-in back porch, where water gurgles along gutters and skylights and tap-taps against its uninsulated roof. I ride the small arc of the double-seated wicker swing back and forth in solitude, listening to the whirs and chirps of peepers, toads, and tree frogs calling out from hidden crevices and damp clumps of dirt beyond the perimeter of the porch. *Solitude.* What a difference a word makes. It's another one of those words—akin to dwell and abide and realm—that speaks to a rich, pacific quality of life, that makes room for the old self to give way to the new one being born. In solitude, there is completeness, a buoyancy in being with one's multi-faceted self. It is so different than feeling alone, or—worse—lonely. When I blow out the candles, a sweet, smoky scent swirls upward to the high-pitched porch ceiling.

It has come to my attention that for a worker bee to produce one pound of wax, it must fly approximately 150,000 miles and visit 33 million flowers. No wonder I don't feel alone. I am floating on the scent of millions of flowers visited by thousands of bees. I revel in the cool, dark air. Solitude gives way to reflection, and I think about what I have made of my life so far—maybe not as impressive or industrious as the bees, but something. Given my limits, constraints, responsibilities, peculiarities, ineptitudes, abilities, genes, and talents—not to mention my rocky start on the cusp of adulthood—I have gathered myself up into this night to do nothing more than ride a double-seated porch swing and feel the hairs at the nape of my neck float up along the glide.

I spend my work days composing online marketing campaigns for nonprofits, strategizing about Facebook postings, website content, blog entries, catchy subject lines and tweets—nothing but micro-bursts of words designed to provoke a caring response and cash donations from the public. But, during my off hours inside The Bird's Nest, I am an old-fashioned "scribbler," one who uses a pen, preferably with some weight and heft, and real paper, with no real ulterior motive. I imagine my true self emerging in the time it takes to curl a descending "g" or make the upward slope of an ascending "h." Writing diary entries in cursive feels counter-cultural. In fact, it may be akin to clinging to Latin during the Renaissance when the rest of the educated European world was putting quill to parchment to express thoughts in the vernacular. In my shed, writing in my journals, I feel more transcriber than writer. I seem to be doing more listening, observing, and recording than actually writing anything creative. The thought has occurred to me that I may simply be taking dictation from the universe.

They fly forward. They fly backward. With two sets of wings, dragonflies hover just above my head and out of reach. Some are so big they could be mistaken for small birds. Despite their versatility when it comes to aerial high jinks, dragonflies cannot fathom that the only way out of an enclosed screened porch is not up. When I find them lifeless on the porch floor after hours of bumping up against the pitched ceiling, I pick them up and bury them amid the red and white impatiens overflowing from my terra cotta pots.

A garter snake has usurped a prime area of the back deck for sunbathing. One day it is coiled in a tidy circle. Another day, it lays outstretched, a conspicuous hump in the middle of its long body. Mouse for dinner? If so, it's one less I have to contend with in my shed. The snake's skin has a tire-tread quality, an olive-green and ivory roping that I think would be fascinating to touch, if I dared disturb its postprandial slumber.

During down times in my work schedule, I ride my bike to Hood Pond, where I jump off the dock and frog-leg back to shore. I pretend to read in the sun, but I am far too busy watching toddlers spoon piles of wet sand into plastic buckets and listening to a nearby group of young mothers complain and kvetch about their husbands' families. One mother is so caught up in listening to the divorce issues of another that she neglects her toddler. A life guard saves her child from an unplanned plunge off the dock. Suddenly, I am no longer relaxed and drowsy. It's time to leave the town pond to the mother-and-diaper set. I am an interloper there.

Forest creep can happen to any house. Vigilance is required of anyone whose house sits on the shoulder of wooded land. I shudder to think what would happen should we abandon our responsibility to our clapboard and brick structure. Tendrils of bittersweet, ivy, and honeysuckle would be the first to entwine themselves into screens, crawl up downspouts, and attach to brick chimneys. It would be downhill after that, with insects invading first, then burrowing animals. We encounter the perils of forest creep during one particularly long New England winter when squirrels decide to invade the family room chimney and homestead at the top of the fireplace damper. When the chimney itself is not commodious enough for all their friends and relations, they bite and scratch their way through the wall, creating a series of smaller condos and access ways. Several even find their way into our house, chasing one another up and down carpeted stairways, leaping from one windowsill to another, chewing window frames in frantic attempts to get outside. All this we discover when we return home from a week in Quebec City. Frank stepped into the master bath to take a shower, only to find himself observed by two beady eyes staring at him from his bathrobe on the back of the door. He managed to jettison the robe— squirrel and all—out the window following frantic attempts on the part of both man and beast to escape each other's company. Forest creep!

Chimney experts, exterminators, carpenters were called in. Several weeks after repairs were finished, I was perplexed by a foul odor in the house. Its source turned out to be a decomposing squirrel concealed under the piano in the family room. I was beside myself with disgust, fuming and fussing over the invasion and the cost to clean up the mess of squirrel tunnels inside the family room wall and the appalling discovery of a forest creature decomposing right under our noses in the family room. Finally, spring arrived, along with warm enough weather to allow the carpenter to return and climb safely up the side of our house to repair extensive exterior damage wrought by the squirrels. As long as he was climbing around on ladders, I asked, could he fix the rotten window casing on the back porch? This brought a fresh bout of forest creep to the fore. "Shut off the electricity!" the carpenter cried, scrambling down from his perch and running with me to the basement to locate the circuit breakers. This time, the invaders were carpenter ants, which had chewed up the inside of the porch wall. They had eaten everything in their way, including the protective rubber coating wrapped around electrical wires, which the carpenter discovered sparking inside rotting wall boards. After frantically calling in an electrician as well as yet another exterminator, that night I blessed the small, furry souls of squirrels that had precipitated the carpenter's visit, possibly saving our house. It turns out you can learn radical gratitude through the most unlikely and unexpected twist of events.

Give me my bike with the wind at my back! Who has the time or inclination to make an Independence Day sheet cake topped with blueberries for stars and strawberries for stripes? Not me! I would rather celebrate the 4th of July pedaling along a coastal road in Maine—and so would Frank and the kids, which is why we head up to Cape Porpoise at the edge of Kennebunkport the day before the holiday. It is cool, overcast, humid, with a flag-snapping breeze and the rush of the ocean's energy pummeling the rocks and sending us reeling backward from the spray. On our bikes, we pedal past harbors and great, churning inlets, turreted mansions, Victorian hotels with expansive front porches overlooking the sea, and the magnificent St. Ann's Episcopal Church constructed from stone on the edge of a cliff. We stop and gape at Walker's Point, site of the Bush family compound, hanging on a jagged promontory at the edge of pounding surf. We continue on to our destination—the Chowder

House at the tip of the Cape—where the harbor is crammed with a fleet of working lobster boats alongside the restaurant and where we order up a couple of seafood platters garnished with a side of fries.

The next day at home in Topsfield dawns gray and threatening. Weather is clearly making its way up the coast. Bethany and Tyler are spending the entire holiday weekend with us, and all of us are on the back porch gazing glumly at the decidedly inappropriate weather that has blown in. A torrential downpour arrives that cancels fireworks in every town along the North Shore and Cape Ann. Frank stands under an oversized golf umbrella as he grills hot dogs and hamburgers on the exposed deck. I set the screened-in back porch table with my homemade potato salad, iced tea, and a pyramid of steaming corn on the cob. The rain thunders through and clears up quickly. After dinner, we pile into the van and drive to Cherry Hill Creamery for ice cream cones before heading to the yacht club, where we ride the launch out to The Flying Dutchman swaying on its mooring. Whispers of clouds drift across a full moon as we wait for the stars to come out. And, then, just when we thought every town in the area had cancelled its fireworks show, it's suddenly Christmas in the sky. Far-off pops and booms and bursts of color float above the tree line across the harbor after all!

I sweep and sweep and sweep some more. The Bird's Nest is an ant graveyard. I reluctantly call the exterminator the day I hear crunching coming from inside the shed's insulated and paneled walls.

Clearly, ants have further infiltrated my tiny and tidy structure, and they are having a feast. It's time to take drastic measures. I need a permanent solution to this problem, since ant traps cannot keep up with the invasion. I dislike the idea of using pesticides, but feel I don't have any choice at this point.

"Oh smell that fresh wood," Mike says as he steps inside The Bird's Nest with his pesticides. "Ants love fresh wood. It's no wonder your little house is under attack."

I am stunned to think that ants have olfactory glands. "Just do what's necessary," I say grimly as I step outside.

A wastebasket has made its entrance into my writing studio. A steel bucket decorated with a pinecone motif, it sits in the corner behind my desk just waiting for discarded thoughts and rejected ideas. Since my inner critic has been banished, I think the waste basket will remain empty for long stretches. Only my artistic companion is permitted inside. She knows enough to be unfailingly supportive and encouraging. She knows that rough sketches and paragraphs can lead to well-developed ideas. She knows that part of me has built this shed at the edge of the ravine in order to feel my way deeper into the mystery, which just may involve a few missteps, misperceptions, and mistakes along the way.

Frank and I sail into Beverly Harbor with the wind at our stern. I go below deck to make tea in an attempt to dispel the chill. A gray blanket of cloud cover has blown up along with an off-shore breeze. It's easy to get the chills on such a day on the open water, but that's not the only reason I am chilled. I want to make myself snug in this small contained space. I want to feel fitted into the universe in some sensible way, as though there is "a place for everything and everything is in its place," as my exacting father used to say. I light the brass gimbaled lantern affixed to the bulkhead and, in the glow of its pale-yellow flame, I drift into memories of childhood. Following on the heels of my sister Sally's recent sudden death, I am attempting to incorporate the premature deaths of both my older sisters in my mind: Ann, who in the late 1960s protested against the discrimination of women at the university she was attending and won the right to enroll in courses previously open only to male students; and Sally, family genius, concert harpist, painter, and free spirit who forged such a brilliant path ahead of me in school that it was difficult to follow in her wake. I try not to feel abandoned. I try to feel my way into the future without them. I am no longer the youngest sister of three. I am now just me, in need of a new way to be.

Frank and I sleep overnight on The Flying Dutchman and awake to watch a heron ghosting by just inches above the water. Although it's daylight, I cannot make out the motorboat that belongs to an engine putt-putting somewhere off our bow. Seagulls are crying and complaining from beyond a layer of gray encircling neighboring boats. Warm air is meeting cold ocean. Fog is everywhere. We are marooned on the mooring; it is too dangerous to set out into the fog-shrouded bay, either toward the docks or out to sea. The weather, I note, is an accurate indicator of my frame of mind. I am shrouded in loss, marooned on my own mooring. Still, it is Sunday morning, and I acknowledge it as a time of reverence and sanctuary, a time to think on a greater reality than the one I am living. As Frank prepares breakfast below deck, I scramble around my purse until I find my miniature *New Testament* and peruse its well-worn pages until I alight on the story of Christ's birth as recorded by Saint Matthew. I am struck by the primacy of dreams in the telling—dreams that impart knowledge, give warnings, secure safety. Joseph, above all, has important dreams that serve to keep Mary and the infant Jesus safe. The three wise men also have important dreams: Don't return to Herod to tell him where they have found the newborn. There's danger and diabolical deeds afoot.

I understand about dreams; my own are as vivid as real life. The night I dream continuously about my sisters and parents—all of whom descend on me in clear disagreement about something— leaves me feeling unsettled. I couldn't understand what anyone was saying, and no one seemed to be listening to me at all. I awoke suddenly and lifted my head to check the time—1:36 a.m. The street number of my childhood home, where we had all once lived together with my three brothers, glowed in neon red numbers against the dark backdrop of the room. Coincidence or synchronicity? Either way, I was stunned. I roused myself from bed and felt my way down the darkened staircase to the kitchen where I processed the strange event with pen and paper:

> *They knock at the door*
> *And ask to be let in;*
> *Is there any keeping them out?*
> *They live in the wind,*
> *In the scent of perfume,*
> *In the aroma of food, in*
> *The melody of song.*
> *Mostly, the night is their domain.*
> *But sometimes they are here*
> *With the dawn of the day.*
> *They come because they appear to*
> *Have something to say:*
> *"We are still here—with you."*

Chapter 9

Heaven is an Unmown Field

The media hype before a hurricane hits is beyond belief. How many swirling bands of color do TV viewers need to understand that "weather" is arriving? First we are told that the storm is lessening, then that it's worsening. At the end of the day, I still don't know if it will hit our shores, or not. I decide to carry on with our Saturday plans and see how things unfold. Frank and I head over to the slopes of Cider Hill Farm in Amesbury, where we pick peaches and apples and more blueberries, abundant and juicy and earthy—a Garden of Eden under an accumulating gray sky and heavy, humid air. We work hurriedly since we are dogged through the orchards by the sense that something is coming. The orchard workers are happy to see us. They have heard a weather update: Batten down the hatches! High winds and rain are on their way even though the center of the hurricane is reported to be spinning out to sea. Still, ripe peaches and apples are sure to be torn from their branches in the melee, and we help gather in as much as we can. The storm has sent an advance man to scope out the landscape. It travels up high in the atmosphere and dulls the sun. There is drama in the waiting. The hairs on our arms rise up on gooseflesh while peach juice runs down our chins. Our fingers are sticky. We dash to the car just in time. Rain pelts our windshield the whole way home. The hyperactive windshield wipers can barely sweep the water away before we're blinded again. What happens overnight is even more fierce. We wake up to thunder and sheets of rain. Dinner by candlelight is one thing, but breakfast by candlelight is another. It's not just gray. It's not just raining. At seven a.m., it's black as night, and torrents of water are pummeling my shed where it sits at the edge of the ravine. I light votives and put them on little flowered saucers on the kitchen island. As I scramble eggs, I look up to watch miniature rivers shift back and forth across the panes of the kitchen window. It is, as the Brits say, a "filthy day."

In fine weather, I go walking. I walk the beach. I walk in towns. I walk along park trails and historic, scenic roads of Topsfield, particularly River Road, where I write a "word snapshot" in my mind:

Heaven is an unmown field.

Wild iris, lupine, tall plumed grasses

Waving in the wind.

White, lavender, bright yellow like a canary.

Heaven is walking up a gentle

Incline along old stone walls and

Egrets gliding along the

Surface of the water, taking shelter in the trees.

Heaven is their silence and

Pumping wings.

Heaven is an unmown field

Bounded by stone and water and sky.

Studded with historic farmhouses, pastures, hedges, lupine fields, horse barns, and grazing sheep, River Road is a world unto itself. Walking or cycling through it reminds me of England's Cotswold region, especially when the day is fine and the sun and winds are soft. Low-slung stone walls upholstered in great swaths of moss dip and rise gently along the road's curves. Walking is a cure for just about any affliction of the spirit I can think of, homesickness for Kansas and my friends there being one. That may explain my penchant for walking. The woods, the beach, historic roads—it almost doesn't matter where I go. Mollie, of course, used to accompany me. She, more than I, understood St. Augustine's abiding wisdom: *Solvitur ambulando.* It is solved by walking.

It is a mouse invasion. The small critters have decided that the long narrow space under my shed's overhang is perfect for establishing a residence, not to mention a nursery. In one week, I rid The Bird's Nest of eight mice—three of them babies I find lolling about on the shed's floor. As cute as they are, I cannot allow the mice to take over my shed. Their scat seems to be everywhere along the shed's ceiling joists and supports. Marilyn sends me a box of balsam needles to scatter along under the shed's front eave. She insists that mice have a particular aversion to the scent, though how she knows this is beyond me. I clean up the mice scat and do as she says with the balsam needles while hoping for the best. The aroma of pine baking under a sun-warmed roof has me dreaming of the Maine woods. For this, I must thank the mice. I must also thank them for the reminder to be on the lookout for forest creep. My small shed could so easily be absorbed into the landscape. I must be vigilant.

At high tide on a summer's eve along the Essex River, Frank and I watch an egret pick its way carefully through the marshes below the deck of the bistro where we are sipping *Pinot Grigio*. Kayakers and motor-boaters glide by on their way to Choate Island and the mouth of the river. There are only so many times we can head to the riverside bistros and clam shacks of Essex for fish and chips. We do it as often as we dare, pushing thoughts of clogged arteries and waist flab into the void. Our favorite is Farnham's. Once only frequented by locals, it has been written up in tourist publications, which means it is no longer hidden on the muddy marsh flats of Essex. Unfortunately for us, it has been found. On a sunny Sunday afternoon in tourist season, we make our way over to Essex to hit the tides in a tandem kayak, putting into the marshes just across from Farnham's. I imagine that our kayaking antics are a great source of entertainment for diners sitting in the window booths we occupy off-season. They stare at us as we stagger under the weight of a double-seated, neon-yellow kayak on the way to the water's edge. The expanse of blue, the marsh grasses, the egrets and herons—on this day all are compliments of Essex County Greenbelt, a local conservation organization which has, for this one afternoon, offered free use of its kayaks to the public. We think we are lucky to have scored the only tandem kayak of the bunch. However, we spend the first hour of our excursion negotiating who would steer and how best to paddle. Our usual boat relationship (i.e. Frank as captain; me as crew) is not working on this particular watercraft. We must renegotiate. On this particular type of boat, Frank is decidedly not always right. In the end, it all comes down to a certain synchronicity, something we manage to attain before our two-hour time allotment in our borrowed kayak is up.

Another day dawns at the edge of the ravine. I hear birds tapping, calling, and whistling. They are flitting back and forth among the tree canopy, alighting on branches, calling out that it's time to begin again. I wake up and think: How amazing would it be to be a bird? It's a challenge to be human. Every day, I rely on underlying ideas and beliefs I barely acknowledge but that I count on to ground me in a creative, compassionate, and hopeful stance. Some days, I confess, I am more grounded and compassionate and certain of who I am and what I believe than others. There must be such comfort (such certainty of mind!) in being an animal outfitted with a pre-programmed identity. There's no casting about, no questioning. No opining or guessing or wringing of hands. Animals and insects are who they are. All is geared toward symbiosis and survival. Beavers build dams. Owls stay on top of the mice population. Flies tidy up the world by eating waste and rotting garbage. They have their assignments. But we humans must always try to figure out how to do the thing we have come here to do. The act of trying can be so trying. No matter how you parse its meaning, trying calls for large doses of stamina.

We have words like epiphany, transcendent, dimension in our lexicon because humans know intuitively that all is not as it appears to be. There is reality underlying this reality that gives rise to hidden knowing, apprehensions of deeper truth, keen perceptions, revelations, and illuminations. Life is not to be taken at face value. If it were, words like epiphany would not be part of our vocabulary.

It's time to toss out lofty reflections and paint Bethany's poetry on a board that I want to hang in The Bird's Nest. One particular poem she wrote is as soul-stirring to me now as it was the day she brought it home from school in seventh grade, a time when she was enchanted by Madeleine L'Engle's *A Ring of Endless Light*—a story that explores interspecies communication between humans and dolphins. Before I hang the poem in its place of honor above the shed's front window, I read it aloud. I want to absorb the words:

If the tides were always gentle,
 If the moon was always bright
If nature was forgiving,
We could see the angels' light.

If all people lived together
In perfect harmony
If we listened to the dolphins
For they surely know more than we.

If we listened to our hearts
Could pursue our true desires,
If humans knew their strength
And kept lit their inner fires.

If a deep but dazzling darkness

Could be seen in everything

If all beings knew what it was to fly

On creation's huge white wings.

Wouldn't it be strange?

"C-R-E-A-K."

I like that the door to my shed announces my arrival and departure. Its hinges could use a douse of household oil, but I let the door have its say. Just as I step inside The Bird's Nest one morning, the sun penetrates the trees to strike a crystal hanging inside the front window. Hundreds of tiny rainbows dance and scatter across the pine paneling and bookshelves along the back wall. The rainbows stay less than a minute before vanishing along with the shifting sunlight. I look around at the artistry of my shed—its red wicker chair and rug, miniature jam jars full of tiny shards of sea glass collected from the beach on Little Misery Island on the window sill. I take in my shed's paneling and ivy molding and mahogany desk gleaming in the sun. I cast my gaze across everything, and think: "I like dwelling here!"

It's a three-quarter moon as The Flying Dutchman bobs on a mooring at Gloucester's Eastern Point Yacht Club. The public is not allowed in, not unless you are a guest of a member or have paid, as we have, for the privilege of staying overnight on one of the club's transient moorings. For $40 a night, any common yachtsman can seek shelter from the elements at Eastern Point, where a heated saltwater pool juts out on a spit of land overlooking an Audubon bird sanctuary and a manicured lawn studded with boulders slopes down to the sea. With its silver tea and coffee urns and polished wood floors, Eastern Point's clubhouse is reminiscent of a mansion from *The Great Gatsby*. Its waters, however, are not optimal for an overnight guest anchorage. In the morning, fishing boats heading out to sea from Gloucester's harbor churn up the club's outer mooring field. Boats tethered to the club's outlying transient moorings tend to pitch and pull on their lines, encouraging all of us visitors to be on our way.

Gloucester's Portuguese Catholic Church—Our Lady of Good Voyage—is topped by a statue of the Madonna holding a Gloucester fishing schooner with one arm. She presides over a city that served as a magnet for 19th-and 20th-century Portuguese, Cape Verdean, and Italian fishermen. Her stance suggests that she is bestowing a blessing on anyone bent on making a living off the Grand Banks. Another statue along the city's waterfront also asks for benediction. An oversized fisherman dressed in old-fashioned oilskins stands at the helm, hand to steering wheel, staring hard out to sea. A scriptural passage—Psalm 107 to be exact—is inscribed at its base: "They that go down to the sea in ships, that do business in great waters. These see the works of the Lord, and his wonders in the deep." Hundreds of names of Gloucester fishermen lost at sea are preserved in a memorial at the base of the statue. On land or sea, the memorial reminds me that we are—and I am—always and forever in need of mercy.

🍃 🍃 🍃

I bike for hours along the recently created Rail Trail, a former railroad line that once connected Boston to Topsfield and points north. Miles and miles of old iron rails were ripped up and the resulting pathway leveled into a workable trail. After years of lobbying, organizing, and investing hours of work clearing weeds and litter, volunteers transformed the trail into a linear park. Plans are to link it up to a trail extending from Maritime Canada to the Florida Keys. On Topsfield's section of the Rail Trail, I routinely skirt the Topsfield Fairgrounds, bounce over the boards of an old railroad bridge spanning the Ipswich River, duck down along a neighboring canal and push past miles of field flowers edging the path. My bike and I flush out cottontail rabbits and free-range chickens from underbrush along the trail. Part of the Rail Trail crosses Route 1, the busy two-lane thoroughfare that bisects Topsfield. Civic-minded people have raised funds to install a flashing light at the dangerous crossing. When I stop to push the signal button, more motorists depress the gas pedal than the brake. I watch them blow by me and think: *Clearly, they do not occupy lives of thoughtful inquiry.*

🍃 🍃 🍃

The moon is not just big. It's mammoth. It's a "super moon." The moon is in its perigee, which means that the full moon appears to be bigger and brighter than any other full moon because it is at its closest approach to the earth during its orbit. I don't know how I could have lived this long without noticing this before, or—for that matter—knowing about this. The moon is so bright that I could be on a stage about to deliver my lines, except that I'm not. I'm standing on our back deck watching the moon cast my shadow across the clearing. In the same week I learn about super moons, I encounter my first "moonglow"—a rainbow surrounding the full moon. During an after-dark nature hike through the Ipswich River Wildlife Sanctuary, our guide points out the shimmering colors encircling the moon. Somewhere out in the dark, surrounding marshes, a beaver slaps its tail on the water's surface. Is it warning other beavers that dangerous interlopers are afoot? Or is it applauding the universe for such an unexpected and spectacular show?

Marblehead Neck is a world unto itself. Connected to the mainland by a causeway that forms the back end of Marblehead Harbor, the Neck is an oasis of well-heeled property owners and stunning water views. It is studded with enormous Victorians topped with "widow walks" and encircled by expansive wrap-around porches. In between, there are renovated modern homes and mansions. There's even a faux French castle overlooking the public path to Castle Rock, as well as what looks like a Spanish *hacienda* with huge cast-iron gates. Tucked in among these behemoths are cottages and tiny "doll" houses on plots no bigger than the houses themselves. Even these unassuming tiny homes are out of our price range. The public park at the highest point on the Neck is open to everyone, whether a resident of the Neck or not, with views both out to sea and across a harbor of yachts belonging to members' of the posh Eastern, Corinthian, and Boston Yacht Clubs. Despite the tony prices and air of privilege, people are friendly. We park our car at the lot adjacent to the public park and walk among the magnificent mansions as we breathe in the scent of the sea. People driving by in BMWs and Mercedes wave and smile at us. They must think we live in the neighborhood, that we are just out for a stroll before cocktails on our verandah overlooking Marblehead Harbor. Anyone can go to the park at the top of the Neck. Anyone can slide down the cliff to its stone-pebbled beach. Anyone can climb its huge granite outcroppings and picnic on its rock-strewn lawn or take 'selfies' at the base of the light tower marking the entrance to Marblehead Harbor, all while surrounded by the roar of the ocean and the smell of the sea. We wave back and smile and nod to everyone we meet on our walks around this privileged place.

The ingredients of our back porch summer suppers never vary. On hot, sultry evenings when I can't stand the thought of cooking, I make what I call my "Supreme Summer Supper"—fresh wheat bread spread with mayo and one enormous slab of heirloom tomato sprinkled with sea salt and ground pepper. For dessert, it's a dollop of black-raspberry sherbet garnished with fresh berries and slivered almonds. Drink of choice? Unsweetened iced tea. The porch ceiling fan must be rotating on high, while an after-dinner nap on the wicker love seat under its circulations is mandatory. In fact, it's all of a piece—a recipe to celebrate summer gladness.

My computer is insisting that I interact with it on a deeper level than I care to. Actually, a food-delivery company's software program is insisting that I interact with it on a deeper level than I care to. When I decide that I no longer want to receive their pre-planned meals delivered to my front door, I am forced to search their website's "Help" menu to find out how to close my account. First, I am required to send an email stating that I no longer want to receive their products. I receive an auto-generated email asking if I am sure I want to discontinue my relationship with the company. If this is the case, then I must click on a link in the email that takes me to the "Close Account" web page on their site. A drop-down menu appears. It wants to know the exact nature of my discontent. Am I offended by the amount of food packaging the company uses? Are the recipes too complicated? Do the meals take too long to prepare? An entire litany of possible grievances appears. There's no "All of the Above," so I click the option that the meals take too long to prepare. A rebuttal pops up on the screen: "It gets easier the more you cook." No, it absolutely does not. I've been cooking daily dinners for decades, and cooking for me has always been tedious. I type in the comments section: "I'm sick of spending so much time in the kitchen." I click the "Close Account" button. An auto-response appears that invites me to return to their convenient meal service.

On the same morning I am forced to jump through hoops at the whim of a pushy meal-delivery company, I call one of my financial institutions to find out why I have received an email confirming that I have changed my phone number in their account files. But I have not changed my phone number, which makes me worried about my account security. I find myself lost in the automatic phone loop, forced to speak to a machine about what I want and the nature of my business. I hang on hold for a good 20 minutes until I finally get connected to a customer service representative who informs me that the institution sent out erroneous email messages to thousands of customers and regrets that this has happened. Did it occur to the institution to send a follow-up email stating that this error has occurred and that all is well? I tell the representative that instead of spending 20 minutes caught in his company's phone loop, I would have preferred being in my sacred shed on the edge of the ravine, and that part of the reason I built it was because I wanted to retreat from the manipulations of large corporations and computer and technology intrusions. I tell him that I am not enamored of this new paradigm wherein machines manipulate people and software answers back like a smart-aleck kid.

As I process these frustrating events at the hands of personal computing, I am reminded that Thoreau and others like him during the late 1800s were desperate to remove themselves from the onslaught and mechanization of factories and other industrial developments. I am reminded that a rural religious retreat house just up the road was founded to provide women and girls laboring in nearby factories of Lawrence and Lowell a Sunday's respite from the grind of their lives and the roar of the machinery. People of that time and place understood that a mechanized world could easily become a dehumanized world, one in which a person's sense of self and relationship with the divine could be obliterated. A world overrun by technology just may pose the same threat.

Outside the sway of our back porch and my shed, I can lose my ability to savor and linger if I'm not careful. I can forego a measured and considered approach to daily life, fail to simply sit and daydream, and stare out the window. If I'm not vigilant, online devices can hijack my inner world and rob me of the serenity I carefully cultivate inside my shed. On a daily basis, I, along with everyone else I know, swipe screens for endless information while rivers of noise rush into my brain. It is relentless exterior hyper-stimulation, manipulation, and insinuation. What has happened to the idea of setting aside time for daydreaming and reflection? Where is the time to arrive at new layers of meaning and insight? In reading about the recent discovery of an abandoned mountain retreat owned by a 19th-century coal baron, I am intrigued by the handwritten "rules" found inside it, pastimes that the industrialist's family had apparently lived by once they crossed the threshold. Those included "knitting in the sun" and "wearing old shoes" while banishing everything from "telephones to ticker tapes and newspapers." I admire them for establishing such firm and intentional boundaries.

Though I appreciate the many qualities, conveniences, and connections my laptop and smart phone afford me, the only screens I allow inside my shed are the kind that keep insects out. Spending time in The Bird's Nest is an antidote to the "busyness" and distractions that plague me elsewhere. It's where I go to remember that my own mind is not, thankfully, the center of the universe. It's where I go to ask: *Will I have time to become all I want to be?* I'm of the mind that everyone should build her or his own sacred shed on the edge of a ravine and spend time inside the mantle of nature. Like Thoreau, I wish to speak a word for Nature. But I also wish to speak a word for Spirit—its ineffable presence that underlies life, enriching it, infusing it with meaning, imbuing it with purpose, with peace, with truth and beauty.

Most of my journals and notebooks consist of spiral-bound sketch books and cheap lined composition books. But there's one in which I record only transcendent moments, experiences, and dreams that shine the light on love as I have come to understand it. Bought in Venice, in a stationers shop at the base of the Rialto Bridge, it is a handmade, thick, leather-bound book with a ridged spine and a round cover plate engraved with the words *Ricordi e Poesie*. Memories and Poetry. "It's too expensive," I said to Frank, even as I took it off a display shelf in the small shop and handled it covetously. "Plus, it seems far too precious for ordinary jottings and entries made on the fly." Just thinking about writing in such a beautifully crafted book felt intimidating. Luckily for me, Frank is deaf to the insidious slings and slandering of my inner critic. He bought the leather-bound journal on the sly, secreted it away in his luggage, and left it for me under the Christmas tree as a surprise. In it, I have recorded as much as I can about the power and presence of love—the gift of the journal from Frank and Frank himself having starring roles within its pages. One particular entry outlines what happened at the bottom of a Mexican cave, or *cenote*, during a family vacation:

Down we went, the kids and Frank and I, clinging to a rough wooden banister, descending 185 wet and slippery circular limestone steps to a fresh water natural pool at the bottom of a cenote. Once we had arrived at the bottom and stood on the ledge of the pool, Frank and the kids were excited about jumping into the dark, bottomless well of water where rubbery-looking, black, eyeless fish circled around the surface. I, however, was intimidated even at the thought of stepping down the slick wooden ladder and immersing myself in the water. I looked around for lifeguards. There were none. Nor did I see any life-saving rings. Instead of leaning into my love of floating, I was paralyzed by fear. That's when I remembered the life jackets for rent we had passed on our way into the park and the accompanying sign: 'It is advisable to wear a life jacket in the cenote.' I groaned. The life jackets were all the way at the top of the 185 slippery steps. And we had brought only the exact entrance fee into the park with us; I didn't have the life jacket rental fee. What to do? With a mixture of regret and deep dismay, I remained on the limestone ledge as my family jumped into the water and swam out to the middle of the natural pool without me. They exclaimed how amazing it was, how good the water felt, how they could look up and see the sky! "Come on, Mom!"

That's when Frank turned and swam back toward me. Without admonishment, without impatience, without complaint or comment of any sort, he hauled himself up the slippery wooden ladder and insisted on climbing back up those 185 slick limestone steps with me, exiting the park, retrieving 30 pesos from his wallet, securing me a life jacket at the rental stand, and descending once again into the bowels of the earth so that I could swim in a natural pool at the bottom of a cave. He coached me down the ladder, encouraged me to let go of its last step, and then coaxed me out into the middle of the pool. The eerie, eyeless, black fish swam along beside us. "Look up," he said, as the sun sliced down an opening in the rock and highlighted the jumping ledge that now seemed even higher than before. I tilted my head back as far as the life jacket would allow. There were jungle vines tumbling down jagged rock walls, flowering roots hundreds of feet long stretching down toward the water's surface, waterfalls splattering across the pool, the great echo of the place, the mystery of what lay beneath my dangling feet, and sunshine piercing a circular hole high above to bathe me in its light. Contained in everything, I saw Frank's unlimited love. I saw that he had simultaneously accommodated my limits while expanding my universe. That's, I think, what love is.

Marilyn's daughter Jane is the only person I know who writes *haiku*, recording the essence of a moment in which nature is linked to human nature. She wrote 65 *haiku* poems to honor her mother's 65th birthday, and as an offshoot of this, Marilyn gifts me with several of the poems hand-written in a miniature book for my own birthday. My two favorites:

At twilight's soft hour,
Poets roam between the worlds
Where all is holy

Colors swirl like spring
Tornados on the prairie
Of your wildest thoughts

I decide to try my own hand at *haiku*, and come up with a few poems which, if not exactly of the same ilk, are akin to the notion:

Seven raspberries
Redolent, rosy, and ripe
Burst into sumptuous song

Chipmunks striped and stealthy
Climb into low-hanging branches
To feast on rubies

In The Bird's Nest, I am not inclined to write poetry. Mostly, I pray, meditate, reflect. I sort through my thoughts. I focus the binoculars and sweep my gaze across the ravine. What am I in search of? And why do I need to take myself away? On some fundamental level, I think I am gathering myself in, rooting in the essence of my identity, re-imagining and recomposing myself into a more vital and vibrant member of the universe as an older woman. It is not lost on me that I am entering a demographic marginalized by society. But I think gifts await me that the younger me would not have recognized or valued. Longfellow has something to say about that:

> *For age is opportunity no less*
> *Than youth itself,*
> *Though in another dress,*
> *And as the evening twilight fades away*
> *The sky is filled with stars,*
> *Invisible by day.*

Something new is being revealed to me on the edge of the ravine, and I cannot hurry it along.

Chapter 10

Life is Short

Every other month, it seems, we talk about the financial benefits of selling our house. Why should we maintain all this superfluous space now that the kids are grown and, for the most part, gone? There are emotional reasons to stay, of course, not the least of which is my newly constructed shed on the edge of the ravine. The ravine itself is a reason to stay. Practical arguments for staying morph into one thought after another, suggesting that downsizing isn't always the answer. There are cautionary tales. There always are. When I bump into older women neighbors at the grocery store they lean in conspiratorially to tell me about their post-children lives. They have ten to 15 years on me. They are grandmothers. Presumably, they have already endured all this middle-aged casting about. One woman tells me that she has already built—and sold— her retirement home on Cape Cod. Widowed just a few months after its completion, she has returned to the town where she and her husband raised their children. "Jim wasn't gone a week when I realized I couldn't live in our dream home all by myself," she tells me. "I stood in the middle of my new spectacular kitchen with its spectacular views and informed the spectacular custom-built cabinets that I was outta there."

Another woman who has remained in her large family house with her husband of 45-plus years cautions me not to be too hasty. "One couple we know sold their house, bought a retirement condo and then ended up becoming guardians of their grandchildren," she says. "They had to buy a big family home and relocate to a good school district all over again! All of that coming and going cost them a pretty penny."

Despite their warnings and my own emotional attachments to our Topsfield property, I continue to roam up and down the coastal towns of Cape Ann to investigate anything that looks remotely affordable near the edge of the sea. The two cottages Frank and I are most interested in are bought up overnight by developers who have the same idea we do—buy a small, somewhat rundown house in a nice neighborhood by the water and renovate. Our realtor Susan tells us we cannot hope to be real players in the real estate market unless we sell our current home first. To do anything else is just flirting with the idea of buying a new house. Are we serious, or not? Exasperated, I hop on my bike and ride the 20 minutes over to Bradley Palmer State Park, where a storybook stone house stands guard at towering wrought-iron gates. The house is not on the ocean, not walkable to a downtown shopping district, and does not have a garage. It does measure up to one prerequisite: It's completely rundown—uninhabitable, to be exact. It's not even up for sale, yet I am completely taken by it. I know that, as in the case of nearby Willowdale mansion, private citizens can take possession of state-owned derelict houses as curators once the properties are restored to their original glory. But I can't imagine how realistic this is for Frank and me. This fairy tale stone structure with shuttered windows and rotting flower boxes is definitely derelict. Its wooden dormer tilts to one side. Its wooden gutters hang by a thread. Its windows are boarded over. God only knows what vermin and varmints have taken up residence. Still, I am entranced. The last time I rode my bike over to the park, a mother and her two small children were play-acting "Hansel and Gretel" in the shadow of the old gatehouse. Clearly, they were caught in its spell, as I am. I straddle my bike as I plot and plan at the edge of the pines, fantasizing about transforming the old stone house into a home. To live there would be to commune with ghosts of industrialists and flappers who paraded through the gates *en route* to parties at Willowdale. Despite the fact that the old gate house has no water views, I think I could be very happy in it. Frank, however, cannot think of tackling such an enormous renovation project, even if the little stone house were available. He wants to know why, when it comes to searching for the possibility of a new home, I am continually drawn to the derelict and down-trodden. I tell him it's because old buildings like the stone carriage house have no equal. They are one-of-a-kind artistry in a cookie-cutter world. They are worthy of renovation and resurrection.

It has been in the high 90s and humid for two weeks straight. Lured by brilliant-red raspberries growing up the side of the porch, I burn the soles of my feet when I step out on the back deck at midday. With our friends Martin and Maureen, who are visiting from Chicago, we decide to make it a water day. In the course of one day, we go bodysurfing at Crane Beach, take The Flying Dutchman out for a short sail across the Sound, and rent canoes along the Ipswich River—my favorite water activity of all. Unlike the glare of the beach and expanse of Salem Sound, the river is a silent, secretive, swirling world unto itself. We glide across reflections of treetops and tangles of vines—an upside-down replica of the world above our heads—and unconsciously tune into an altered time zone where turtles lounge on logs, garter snakes slither at the river's edge, red-winged blackbirds flit among overhanging branches, and dragonflies and damselflies skim along the surface of the water. Most damsels I spot are a stunning iridescent blue. A large red dragonfly escorts us along the river, perhaps wanting to land for a rest on one of our shoulders, but thinks better of it and flies off. Since we have come from the salt of the ocean's waves, we decide to beach the canoes on Perkins Island and rinse off in the current.

Our sailing excursions on The Flying Dutchman frequently end up at the protected inlet between Little and Big Misery Islands at the edge of Salem Sound, where we ride the inflatable dinghy into the small rocky beach on Little Misery. I find sea glass of all sorts: A rare azure-blue chip polished to perfection, along with dozens more that are mostly white or dull brown. My blue piece—I can't decide if it's more azure or sapphire—is the treasure of the day. I also collect small shells: Pearl-like shards with bits of shiny lavender coverings, some the size of small tea biscuits with a little half shelf on the underside. It's hard to resist picking up miniscule bright yellow periwinkles—my favorites—that seem to be too tiny to ever have been part of such a massive, heaving ocean.

Every trip to the Miseries includes a short walk up a path on Little Misery that's studded with pine cones and wild daisies (not to mention patches of poison ivy) to the top of a ridge engulfed in underbrush. A parting of branches, and we emerge onto a cliff that plummets to a restless, brooding surf raking across stones that make a racket bouncing off one another. We gaze across the channel to Baker's Island lighthouse. There is something supremely satisfying about standing atop one island to look across the cut to another of such picturesque proportions. "Say it," says Frank, knowing that I can't help myself. It's a thought that comes to the fore every time we stand at a particularly arresting natural landscape: "It's either heaven or Hollywood. I can't decide which." My voice trails off into wonder. Crashing surf, ragged cliffs, a circular lighthouse with red-roofed houses clustered at its base—the scene is so emblematic of New England that it begs to be preserved inside a bottle.

We decide to spend the night on anchor between the two islands. I can't imagine why I choose to read travel magazines in the cockpit before we descend into the cabin to prepare for bed. Why would I want to dream about any other destination? I look up from the glossy pages splashed with photos of couples cavorting on beaches and roaming through a rain forest. I lift my head to see mauve and pearl-pink ribbons of sky bleeding into an ocean pulsating with pastels. The gong buoy on the other side of Big Misery ca-langs and bangs back and forth erratically in a choppy sea. After sundown, an iridescent full moon rises along a watery path between Big and Little Misery. Only four other sailboats appear to be over-nighting with us. One by one, their white anchor lights turn on at the top of masts. Cabin lights illuminate the water surrounding our hulls. We toast the rising moon and retreating summer. The shush of the tide surging into the cut between Little and Big Misery is our night music. A seagull flying in low across the front deck sounds like the faint rustle of taffeta, and there is a splash of phosphorescence in the water that's winking and twinkling like miniature underwater fireworks. Before we go below, we are surprised to see a "V" of eight white herons in formation, their feathers illuminated in bright moonlight, shooting like arrows across the night sky.

I take my bike out on a final solo summer spin through Bradley Palmer State Park, along Highland Street in Hamilton, where row after row of cornstalks wave at me from fields that dip and crest into gentle rises encircled by woods. As I pass, I bid *adieu* to the halcyon days of summer. These surrounding fields are nothing like the endless Kansas farm fields we drove along on our way from Overland Park to Lake Perry in Kansas, where Frank had to content himself with mooring The Flying Dutchman during our, as he says, "landlocked years." Still, the rolling fields provide peace and abundant space to rest my soul. I pedal on toward the pastures and dirt roads of Appleton Farms. Crickets chirp unseen among the weeds and wildflowers while grasshoppers hurl themselves up and over long-stemmed grasses. I stop to admire two "stone men" at the entrance to the Farms. They look just like snow men, but have been made from boulders, one stone in diminishing size stacked atop the other. On my way home, I bump into my friend Sheila who is on her own '*sayonara* summer' bike ride. She takes me deep into the back dirt trails and former carriage roads of Bradley Palmer. "Is it safe?" I ask, slightly alarmed by signs that warn of packs of coyotes roaming the park. Sheila, clearly, is not as spooked as I, and leads the way through stands of forests and across gentle meadow swells as the sun casts long striped shadows of tree trunks across the land. We bask in the golden light and vow to remember this moment during the long dark days of winter ahead.

The impossibly long gravel drive, the curve of the land falling away and blending into neat stone-walled gardens, gazebos, out-buildings, barns, and a riot of rhododendrons—I can't be anywhere else but at the magnificent industrialist-era Crane Estate at Castle Hill in Ipswich. The Atlantic Ocean lies just beyond the undulating landscape of the property's expansive manicured lawn known as the *Grand Allée*, and when I roll down the car window, I can smell its presence, even if I can't quite hear the surf. The lights on either side of the mansion's enormous front door are ringed with yellow haloes in the drizzly dusk of twilight. I'm not here for a tour or to attend some swanky black-tie fundraiser. I'm here to learn how to make beach plum jelly, of all things. The Trustees of Reservations, the organization that now owns and maintains this magnificent property, runs canning workshops out of the mansion's magnificent kitchen, and eight other women and I are going to "put up preserves" in a kitchen the size of a concert hall.

For some reason, known only to wind and tide, beach plums are scarce this year. But, our instructor assures us that the beach rose, otherwise known as *rosa rugosa*, produces bright red seed pods called "hips," (often confused with the dark purple plums) and can be used to make jelly through a process similar to making fruit jellies. Consequently, our Beach Plum Canning Workshop has turned into a Beach Rose Jelly Canning Workshop. None of us in the class are fazed by this. We confess that we can't tell the difference between a rose hip and a beach plum. It's just fun to be in the mansion after hours, in an immense kitchen with Delft-blue tiles marching up and down the walls and an expansive porcelain sink and counter running the length of an entire wall. It's fun pretending to be a servant in a grand house in such surroundings, though I'm sure the reality of that life was taxing. In between the clipping of rose hips and boiling of water, our instructor takes us on a backstairs tour of the mansion, to places the servants would have frequented and fled to in their off hours. There is a lot of standing around and waiting that goes along with the art of canning, and this foray into the world of the servants helps pass the time. By the time the "hips" have boiled into a sticky mass and the jars have been sterilized and the entire concoction has had its 10-minute turn in a boiling bath and the rings on the jars have popped and sealed properly, we are done. We each take home a mini Mason jar of amber-colored rose hip jelly. The fruit has boiled down into very little mass, but it turns out to be delicious on homemade wheat toast at breakfast the next morning.

Green Meadows Farm is only a stone's throw from our house, and I have it in mind to partake of their end-of-the-summer Farm-to-Table outdoor feast—until, that is, I learn that lamb is on the menu. "Not lamb!" I practically shout into the telephone when I call to make reservations. How could they serve up something that only last spring they had invited the public to coo and fawn over at their "Meet and Greet" open house? Even if I weren't already a vegetarian, I doubt if I could take a bite of something I had watched frolicking in the farm's fields. As much as I would like to sit at wooden benches in the dusk of a waning summer twilight and eat a communal meal at a candle-lit table strewn with field flowers, I cannot. No. I make my apologies to the woman on the other end of the phone and decline to make reservations.

Sitting at my desk on the lip of the ravine, overlooking the forest and wetlands below, my thoughts flow from mind to hand to pen. I interact with something as ordinary as a grape stem plucked of its fruit. I investigate its ins and outs, its small claw-like formations, its tiny stems at the tip of its "branches." I do what is known in the artistic realm as a 'searching inquiry.' I begin to sketch its form. As I watch it replicate on paper from the tip of my 4B pencil, I see that the stem was dancing as it developed, bending first this way and then that, following a creative impulse.

Suddenly, it occurs to me that where I am dictates who I am. In my writing shed, it's easy to feel at ease, intent on seeking and giving forgiveness, feeling tolerant of others' and my own shortcomings. Am I the same person sitting in traffic inside one of Boston's notorious "Big Dig" tunnels where I have been known to fuss and fume and honk and glare? It occurs to me that I must carry the "me" of my Bird's Nest into the larger world. It occurs to me that, in building my writing shed, I have created my own alternative universe, a place where a larger vision holds sway. I leave the world behind and enter a place where a reorientation and an alternate reality takes hold, where a more expansive reality reigns. After time there, I return to the world ready for the fray once again. The rituals of a Japanese tea ceremony inside a tea house is said to hold much the same power; its "way of *chanoyu*"—the intentional creation of a space and attention to the smallest detail in order to bring to mind underlying universal principles of harmony, respect, purity and tranquility—seems to provide a similar reorientation. A Japanese tea ceremony, retreating into my shed—both are intentional practices of stepping beyond daily attachments, corrosive habits, and ways of thinking to cultivate a more creative and life-giving way of being in the here and now, where every passing moment slips into the past even as it is actively lived.

I discover Kakuzo Okakura's classic, *The Book of Tea*, during a foray to Boston's Isabella Stewart Gardner Museum and am completely taken with it. It is not really about tea, of course, except that tea serves as the conduit to a more expansive view of the universe and the individual's transformation within time and space. It is said that Mrs. Gardner encouraged Okakura to write a treatise about cultivating awareness of deeper truths through the rituals of his native Japanese tea culture. In the early 1900s, the fabulously wealthy art collector Mrs. Gardner and Okakura were great friends, perhaps even spiritual companions. She was in the enviable position to act as a patron of sorts for him, opening doorways into her Boston Brahmin world while he introduced the essence of the Asian mindset and accompanying artistic rituals to her world. In one of the smaller exhibit rooms off the museum's soaring courtyard, I push aside a protective piece of brocade fabric concealing artifacts inside an old-fashioned glass museum case. Underneath the protective brocade is an original black-and-white photo of Okakura robed in traditional Japanese dress, along with one of his slender paint brushes, and a poem he had written for Mrs. Gardner in flowing black ink—artifacts of a relationship that evaporated long ago.

Fall arrives with a bang! The ravine is in an uproar. High winds sweep treetops sideways, huge limbs crash and fall into smaller trees below. Two deer lumber into the deeper area of the ravine and barge their way through overhanging vines and branches. A multitude of birds sets up a raucous din from concealed perches while a flock of starlings packed in tight formation swoops one way and then another, taking off and landing in uniformity of movement, as if it is a school of fish in the sky. On the other hand, the frogs fall silent, or maybe they are just drowned out by the racket of everything else seeking cover from the coming storm. It finally arrives: Teeth-rattling thunder boomers—what we used to attribute to "angels bowling in heaven" when I was a kid—and spears of lightning. And then torrents of water released from the sky.

Kate has told me that she thinks my animal totem is a robin redbreast—not a groundhog that Jane swears by—which could be true, I suppose. Given the number of robins that visit me on a regular basis, and their extraordinary interest in the construction of my shed, I would not be surprised. I wonder if it's possible to have more than one animal totem at the same time? If so, I'd be delighted to have a special relationship with a robin. I especially like the meaning attributed to their totemic powers: This tiny bird is said to escort spirits on their way to new life.

Just when I think I have adjusted to this post-Mommy life and part-time work and writing schedule, I am offered a job—a good job, a full-time job, downtown Boston. I must accept it. It's what I've been searching for since the kids moved out of the house. A renewed sense of purpose! People will count on me! There will be camaraderie! And an increased sense of professional prestige! I go out to The Bird's Nest to give it the news that I will be spending long days commuting in and out of town and long days in an office doing things other than ruminating in my shed's embrace and recording my days in blank notebooks, though any spare time I have will be spent doing just that. I tell it that the job won't last forever, that it's only a temporary contract, that I'll soon enough be back to wondering about the new me emerging in this evolving life.

I ride the commuter rail into my new job in town, and—true to my word—make my way out to The Bird's Nest after I return home at dusk to write by candlelight. It is a joy to have this balance, to be restored by solitude while also having the stimulation of new work in the city. I am hoping that one world will inform and temper the other. To write by the glow of a candle flame as hundreds of tiny, whirring insects announce sundown just outside my window is transporting. The stress I have carried with me throughout the day is released through the flow of ink on paper as I move my hand across the page of my journal. I can't imagine that insects or songbirds suffer from anxiety or any sort of existential afflictions and worries. I can't imagine that they go to sleep only to be awakened by bad dreams. I am currently obsessing about work deadlines—an alien concept within my shed world.

A lone chipmunk is making a racket "chipping" in the ravine, and I wonder if it's chafing under its own limits. I locate it with my binos and watch its small hunched body perched in the crotch of a downed birch; its front paws are clasped together, as if in prayer, as if beseeching someone—God, anyone—for aid, enlightenment, mercy. Burdened by new expectations and, as of yet, undefined work relationships, I find myself commiserating with the little creature. What comes to mind is a prayer written by 19th-century Frenchman Henri Frederic Amiel, which I first heard during lunch-time prayer services at Trinity Church Boston. I spontaneously superimpose the prayer over the chipmunk's syncopations so that we perform a type of duet, the chipmunk and I:

Life is short;

(Chip – chip – chip – chip)

And we do not have too much time

(Chip – chip – chip – chip)

To gladden the hearts of those

(Chip – chip – chip – chip)

Who travel the way with us.

(Chip – chip – chip – chip)

So be swift to love and make haste to be kind...

(Chip – chip – chip – chip)

(Chip – chip – chip – chip)

(Chip – chip – chip – chip)

I eventually leave the chipmunk to its supplications. At the moment, it is clearly imbued with greater zeal than I.

On occasion, *The New York Times* prints an accounting of American troops killed overseas, accountings that include the ages, ranks, and hometowns of the fallen. The casualty reports are edged in black, easy enough to notice if a reader is looking for them, easy enough to ignore if not. I retreat to my shed to read their names and particulars aloud. I especially linger over the names of those in their 20s who are gone before they had a chance to live. I pray for their mothers and fathers, their families, their lovers, and any children they may have left behind. Though we are strangers, I place my hand across the page and call each soldier to mind. I guess at nicknames:

Bob or Robbie for Robert. Woody for Woodruff. Nick for Nicholas. I glue the lists of names to a page in my journal and collage paper cutouts in the shape of tears around their black edges. During a walk at Crane Beach, I find a teardrop-shaped gemstone— a lost earring perhaps?—tossed up by the tide. I glue that to the page as well so that the collage becomes 3D. As I do so, I am surprised to feel soldiers in battle fatigues crowding around my desk. They want to know who is calling them to mind.

What is this connection I seem to have to fallen soldiers and war memorials? My own life has been touched only tangentially by war: My father's service as a fighter pilot in training during WWII, my mother's terror at the possibility of my oldest brother being drafted during the Viet Nam War. Nonetheless, I make it a point to seek out war memorials—a mainstay of every New England town common and prominent intersection. Civil War memorials, especially, take center stage. In Ipswich, at one such spider's web of intersecting roads based on former cow paths, town officials had erected a tall granite obelisk to commemorate the fallen in the faraway battlefields of Antietam and Gettysburg. Young men bearing such 19th-century names as Luther Andrews and Caleb Lord are immortalized in stone. On the memorial, they are described as "brave and lamented sons" who gave their lives for the Union and liberty. As the only visitor to the memorial on a beautiful sunny afternoon, I wonder if there is anyone in town who thinks on the sacrifice of these young men, if their descendants ever sit and call them to mind.

In the South, there are entire battlefields devoted to memorializing the war dead from both sides of the Civil War. On heat-dazed days, when the air presses against the earth and a staggeringly hot sun stuns every life form but cicadas into silence, the southern landscape still vibrates with battle. As newlyweds who moved to Virginia in the early 1980s, Frank and I sensed the pulse and immediacy of that war even 120 years after it had ended. At that time, as they plowed their fields, farmers in the area were continuing to unearth bullets from the conflict. They found so many that they sold bullets by the bucketful alongside bins of summer squash and heirloom tomatoes at their farm stands. On the way home from a visit to Manassas National Battlefield Park, I stopped at one such farm stand and bought a handful of the heavy dull-white projectiles for 50 cents each. They remain in my possession to this day, clearly significant in some way I cannot quite name.

To awaken to burnished gold reflected into our bedroom window from the ravine below is bliss. So is going out to The Bird's Nest (on a work morning, no less!) to say hello to the day. I throw open all its windows in the mild Indian summer air, which sets the shed's Japanese tea garden bell to tinging and ringing in the breeze. The slant of the autumn sun infuses my little house with a bright honey-colored light. I am enfolded inside the arch of overhanging tree branches. Spiritual writer Joyce Rupp writes about sitting inside a hollowed-out space at the base of a 1,000-year-old tree in Spain during her pilgrimage along Spain's Way of St. James. She rested there, encased in the tree's energy, wearing the mantle of its solemn presence around her shoulders like a shawl. How amazing would that be—to sit inside the trunk of such a tree?

The gift of the day occurs not inside the shelter of a tree or inside my writing shed, but during a walk to the marshes of the Audubon sanctuary along Perkins Row, where I follow a boardwalk through a sea of cattails. There is something reassuring, so tidy and orderly, about making one's way along a perfectly circumscribed trail. The cattails' brown bonnets at the tip of their tall, slender stalks are exploding; they look like unraveling skeins of brown wool. Tufts of billowy, white seeds also rise up from the marshes like fairies on the wind and glimmer in the sunshine. They waft along on invisible currents, performing a dance.

"Accomplished" is a word the ego loves. It's not a word of the spirit, nor is it a word I associate with my shed. I am not intentionally accomplishing anything while sitting at my mother's old mahogany desk and gazing out across the ravine. I am abiding. I have discovered a man in Bar Harbor, Maine, who has built what he calls a "tiny cathedral"—nothing more than a shed constructed of stone—in his search for, as he says, "love and wonder." The act of abiding may just lead to their discovery. Is there anything anywhere more worthy of being sought?

It's that time of year when I walk past a simple bush, something no more than a ground shrub, and I am stunned by its appearance, its apparition of color. It is suddenly vibrant, rip-roaring RED, when only a few weeks earlier it was the color of mud. But now it has transcended itself. There is magic in the passage of the earth's rotational journey, enchantment in the turn of the tides. Green becomes red and yellow, ochre and orange. Red is the new brown. Nothing is as it once was.

The clay tiles I pressed with forms of sea shells and nuts and fired in Marilyn's pottery kiln are finally mounted in a frieze above the interior doorway of the shed. Though I love the natural motif, my favorite tile is the one I imprinted with a bird stamp I found among Marilyn's studio tools, and which I then glazed with an eggplant-color wash before firing. The tiny aubergine bird is singing inside a wreath of holly leaves—another fitting bird motif for The Bird's Nest.

I have a propensity to build altars. It's an easy enough pastime on Crane Beach at a particularly low tide. All I need are a few scattered broken shells, pieces of gnarled driftwood. One day, I found a jagged-edged horseshoe crab shell encrusted with tiny periwinkles and other shells, along with an enormous rotten beam (from a dock or ship?) that had washed ashore at the mouth of the Essex River. The beam served as a perfect base for my altar to the sea. As I worked at my construction, a gentle "shushing" of waves whispered prayers along the shoreline. My own prayers have evolved over time, thankfully becoming less ego-centric and more expansive. I no longer make unreasonable demands or request certain outcomes of God, as I did on a regular basis when I was young. Like writer Anne Lamott, "help," "thanks," and "wow" have pride of place in my personal prayer department, though there are times when I succumb to "That can't be right!" Or "You have got to be kidding me!" In my more articulate (and measured) moments, I ask how to best express and enact love, especially when challenged and stressed by people I find difficult to accommodate. On a beautiful day at the beach, prayers are easy enough to come by. It's not hard to feel unified with such a pacific seascape. All I have to do is breathe in and out in concert with the gentle surf. But I must be careful. If I'm not paying full attention, prayers can sometimes devolve into brooding. Early September always vibrates with the loss of summer, but there is far greater loss associated with this time of year. As I head for home, I have an insight somewhere between mounting the dune steps on the beach and descending them on the other side to the parking lot: Brooding is not constructive.

While having breakfast with sparrows on a beautiful early September morning at an outside café on Newbury Street before heading to the office, I send silent greetings to my mother on what would have been her 93rd birthday. "Birthday greetings, Betts," I say, as I enjoy a croissant with strawberry jam and a pot of English Breakfast tea. It feels strange to address her by name, but at this point, "Mom" sounds childish, an artifact from another century, if not another life. I have lived part of my youth and my entire adult life without her. Sparrows fly in low and flutter at my feet; they are collecting crumbs from my croissant. Some are so bold as to hop along the edge of the tabletop. I am so pleased that they have come to be with me. As they cock their little heads questioningly, I divulge a secret that has lain dormant for decades: "Life," I confide to their earnest little faces, "demands strength of soul."

Chapter 11

Death without Dying

Why do I assume that only one thing can be true about a particular event or situation when I know that life is multi-dimensional? My shed is a case in point. The mice think I have constructed it for their nesting purposes. The birds assume I have built it as a landing pad and place of rest along the roofline. The wasps have usurped its front overhang as a windbreak for their papery nests. Small woodland creatures use the slight gap between the shed's under-flooring and the ground as a safe way-station between our back clearing and the ravine. And, despite the fact that I thought I was primarily building my shed to reflect on the numinous quality of nature, I am beginning to notice that hidden truths and past lives are emerging in my sacred shed here on the edge of the ravine. How is it that a structure built with reflection and solitude and rest in mind has become so freighted with purpose?

🍃 🍃 🍃

"Dada!"

Pause.

"Mommy!"

On a summer afternoon, the high-pitched voices of the small boys who live across the ravine pierce my concentration as I write in my shed. Their voices—so precious, so vulnerable, so small— transport me to Virginia, where Frank and I started our family and where I doted on our own small children. Suddenly, my mind is awash with images of me cradling Bethany and Tyler on my shoulder, patting their little backs, hoisting them up on my hip, washing their small food-smeared faces as they struggled and whined and squirmed to be free. The minute I open my mind to memories, I am leaping across decades. I'm a college student studying English Romantic Poetry while working as a bakery cashier on weekends and traipsing around Europe during summer breaks with Frank. I'm a full-time communications professional in Washington, D.C., wearing suits and high heels to business meetings, a young wife awash in the challenges of new motherhood, a middle-aged freelance writer driving teens around to soccer practice and choir rehearsals during my part-time enrollment at Weston Jesuit School of Theology. All my selves visit me in my shed at one point or another.

The child me is the first to make her appearance. She reminds me that being enamored with nature and solitude is a consistent expression of my essence. She reminds me that as a child I was entranced by earthworms, even kissing their dirty little heads when they came up for air after a spring rain. She trots out the collie dogs named Ping and Pong—so like Mollie—who lived across the street. It was Pong I adored, petting and hugging him for hours as we sat on his front lawn in between Wiffle-ball games, roller-skating up and down the street, and racing go-carts around the neighborhood. She reminds me that even then, as an eight or nine-year-old, I understood about the transitory nature of life. Together, she and I revisit what I came to call my "Christmas telling," when I intuited that the life my family and I were living inside the arms of our grand old Victorian house would not last. The "telling" happened quite suddenly, barging in from left field, as my mother was pounding out a jazzy rendition of "Deck the Halls" on the piano in the bay of the dining room, and my siblings and I along with assorted others celebrating Christmas Eve with us were gathered around, singing raucously and ringing bells and banging on tambourines. In the middle of all that merry-making, a window flew open in my mind. Suddenly, I was on the outside looking in. At that moment, I perceived that we were nothing but a passing show; I understood perfectly that it would be ending. I was shown how transitory life is, how transitory life is meant to be. Tears flew to my eyes, and I crept unnoticed toward a corner of the dining room away from the raucous singing to ponder this strange event. I told no one of this revelation. In short order, I hid it away in my mind, in what I came to call my "top secret" file.

The degenerative heart disease that robbed my mother of life a few years after my "Christmas telling" did not prevent her from being interested and involved in the unfolding dramas and developments of my life and those of my siblings for as long as she could. After the difficult onset of her illness when I was a scant four years old, she managed to remain remarkably resilient and engaged in life, as long as she took her digitalis-based heart medicine along with a daily afternoon nap. Even so, there were setbacks and anxieties, all of which I absorbed as part of the reality of our family. Since this illness was normal for our family, I assumed every family had its own issues and illnesses. Mental retardation had afflicted a boy down the street. Next door there was alcoholism and cancer. The police frequently arrived at the house across the street, so something upsetting was happening there. Something else, I knew, was wrong with Dave the mailman, but I didn't know what. We would all, nevertheless, overcome whatever was hindering us from wholeness and happiness, wouldn't we? My "Christmas telling" caused me to question that we would.

As is the case with the unruly mice, the industrious wasps, and the army of ants, there seems to be no sure-fire way to keep all my selves at bay. Following the final placement of the tiles over the shed's doorway, after the last whack of the hammer died away, after all my tools are returned to their assigned storage boxes in our basement, and I am convinced that the construction of my shed is finally and forever finished, more versions of myself begin making curtain calls. Their appearances coincide with the approaching completion of my temporary work contract downtown Boston, which is no doubt making me anxious and uncertain. Before I know it, former selves are inviting themselves into The Bird's Nest and taking a seat in its red visitor chair. Apparently, they, too, think I have constructed my shed for their benefit. Perhaps I have. Perhaps it's time to integrate them all more fully into my larger self and be done with it. Perhaps, with the help of the memories they carry, I will find my way into yet another way of being me.

My 16-year-old self is particularly insistent on getting some face time. I can't imagine what she could possibly want at this stage of the game, and—quite frankly—I'm not all that happy to see her. In fact, I've kept her at bay for decades. My life is so much richer, so much larger, so much more grounded—so much more joyful and less fearful—than when I was her. But, clearly, she is here because she has something to say. True to form, she is as straightforward as ever: *Without being me, you never would have come to understand the depth of your light.* In my heart of hearts, I know she is right, though I am still not wild about having her visit. I can't overlook the fact that the foundation of my entire womanhood rests squarely on her slight shoulders. She insists on pulling out my "top secret" file that contains memories I would just as soon forget. She makes it very clear that I would not be living my current life without her fortitude and stamina. She is the one who endured the unexpected freefall and fallout of my 16th year. She is the one who stood firm and mustered the courage to penetrate the darkness so deep that there was nowhere to go but up. She is the one who was able to grasp that there was light down there somewhere and that she would persevere until she found it. I have gone to great lengths to deny her access to my subsequent happy life, but now I think it may be time to give her her due. She is asking me to reassess my view.

The truth is I survived my sixteenth year hanging on by a thread. It wasn't only that I had spent the entire summer between my sophomore and junior year of high school in high anxiety, first hovering at the side of my mother's hospital bed and, then, reeling from shock at her graveside that September. It was also living on a daily basis for years with the low-level anxiety of both knowing and not wanting to know about the inevitable outcome of my mother's illness. It was about sudden parental role reversals, about encountering the reality of death up close and personal for the very first time, about having to let go of someone I loved and couldn't imagine living without when every fiber of my body, heart, and soul was screaming to hang on. It was a seesaw event. First my mother was failing, then she appeared to be rallying. It was impossible to predict how a day would unfold. No adult took me and other younger siblings aside to tell us what was what. We were left to eavesdrop, glean bits of information from conversations overheard at the nurse's station or during my father's one-sided telephone conferences with doctors. We were left to stare at beeping machinery displaying inscrutable numbers and squiggly lines, all apparently measuring fluids and functions through tubes and wires attached to my mother's body. It was completely inexplicable—unknowable— to my sister Sally and me as we rubbed lotion onto our mother's swollen feet, fed her ice chips, and read aloud to her from one of her favorite suspense novels and piles of get-well cards every afternoon. One day, she took a drastic turn for the worse: Our mother failed to recognize us when Sally and I arrived in her hospital room.

The next day, we returned to find our mother lucid, but exhausted. She didn't remember our visit from the day before, but she did remember a remarkable dream she had had, wherein she was presented with three doors to walk through. She needed to decide which one she would open. Overwhelmed by choice, she had hesitated in front of all three doors and told us that she awoke from the dream still uncertain as to what her choice should be. What door should she open? Despite all the flowers, best wishes, and get-well cards coming her way, at that moment I knew that my mother was never going to get better, and that she knew this as well. She had known this all along. I was unable to imagine what would come next.

On any given day, my mother was called upon to mollify my father. His irritable and resentful outbursts about any number of things large and small appeared to be rooted in some deep wound suffered during childhood. He conveyed the attitude that he was justified in behaving in this manner and exempt from having to make apologies on account of this wounding. As a young man returning from WWII, he had chosen my mother—a young woman rooted in the austere and exacting Roman Catholic Church of the 1930s—as his wife, when he himself operated in the world without any sort of overarching religious orientation, a Protestant of no particular persuasion who had needed special dispensation to marry my mother in the "one true church." It was a decision that kept him forever teetering along a continuum of financial uncertainty, as one child after another came on the scene, never allowing him to fully shake the dark days of hunger and want of the Great Depression embedded in his tissue memory.

With this as the reality, there was no way my father (or we kids, for that matter) would emerge unscathed from the experience of my mother's lengthy hospitalization and death. He rallied and failed right alongside her. The only problem was that he was left to do the final rallying when he had no idea how. She had always been the one to comfort and reassure him, and when he needed her the most in this regard, she was not there. The truth is none of us were prepared for the finality and fallout of her death. We all pulled disappearing acts of one sort or another. I can vouch for the fact that, as we gathered around my mother's graveside and watched her casket lowered into the oblong hole in the ground, there was no "me" in me. Someone inhabiting my skin watched our family priest spray an arc of holy water across the casket and commission my mother's soul to the Great Lord of All. At the time, I thought what a foolish gesture that was. There was no way on earth tiny drops of water, a chemical compound that would evaporate inside a minute, could carry anything holy or sacred into eternity. I turned away from my mother's burial in fury and grief, resolving there and then never to have children of my own. I retreated into a spiritual wasteland, exiled in fear.

The god I grew up with in the 1960s Catholic Church was not one for mucking about in life's losses. God the father was male, of course, emotionally inaccessible and easily angered. This god did not descend from "his" heavenly throne to take the seat next to me in the intensive care waiting room as my mother lay dying down the hall. This god didn't show up at her graveside. This god was secreted away behind heavy velvet curtains of the dark confessional. This god demanded to be kept apart from the fray of human existence, mediated through polished chalices and Communion patens, stained-glass windows, delicate lacework draped across marble altars, and by male priests ensconced behind satin robes embroidered with gold thread. This god didn't even speak English; Latin was "his"

native tongue. As far as I could tell, there was no comfort or inspiration forthcoming from this god. (What creator would actually want to fraternize with creatures oozing original sin?) And "he" was guarded on "his" throne in heaven, as the Sisters of Saint Joseph had informed us second-graders preparing for First Communion in the spring of 1963, by several layers of angels encircling the earth—something that soon made no sense to me as I watched Apollo space flights blast off from Cape Kennedy on my family's black-and-white TV. Perhaps the most devastating attribute of this god was that "he" especially disliked females. I could only assume that this god disliked me. At age 16, I consigned the entire construct of the god I grew up with to the dustbin. I pushed myself off from the shores of an inherited, stultifying religion that was bent on emphasizing my sins and need for the sacraments of the institutional church in order to make amends and be saved. I pushed off into uncharted and terrifying territory.

It has occurred to me that I have been enamored by biographies and historical diaries, letters, and journals of strangers' lives for as long as I can remember because I have so little personal historical context of my own. Genealogical research tells me nothing. It's no more than who "begat" whom, an empty exercise since I don't have any stories to associate with my ancestors and no one to ask. My immediate family of origin had operated in its own rarified sphere, according to its own rhythms. We were an island unto ourselves, somehow "better," more enlightened and advanced than our relatives and ancestors; we were part of the post-World War II newly educated American middle class. We were supposedly upwardly mobile. The relatives left behind in Minnesota and Washington did not participate in our family structure in any meaningful way. We had no cousins to play with, no aunts or uncles who sat around our old wooden kitchen table drinking coffee on a Saturday evening and playing cards. No grandparents who came to see us kids in school plays or visit at holidays. Following my parent's wedding in the late 1940s, my father's doctorate degree—compliments of the GI Bill—opened doors to professorship posts that took him and my mother farther and farther from their childhood homes and past lives and all the people part of those lives. Along the way, my mother helped advance my father's academic career by becoming active in the Faculty Wives' Clubs at the universities where he taught, until he hit the jackpot as a tenured professor on the East Coast. But all these progressions of travel and employment weakened their ties to family roots until it seemed that there really were no roots at all. We were a family without extended familial connections, void of extenuating stories—all of which meant that, in a crisis, we were a family without wise elders to assure us of their support and alleviate my father's burden.

During this time of disorientation and spiritual chaos, Marilyn, who was living next door and crafting pottery on her kick wheel while raising four small children, was a source of sustenance and strength. In untold wisdom and compassion, she grounded me in life's underlying creative rhythms. On my worst days, she took my hands in hers and taught me to weave on a small loom in her kitchen. She included me at her kitchen table with her small daughters to craft pinecone wreaths. She gave me access to her pottery studio and encouraged me to mold and shape clay. On countless evenings, when I would walk into her house uninvited because I couldn't imagine what else to do with myself, her family—including Pippin the cat and ancient black Lab Spooky—quietly moved over to make room for me in front of their kitchen's wood-burning stove, while Marilyn would offer me homemade doughnuts or apple pie she had baked that afternoon. Her husband Tom would take out his guitar and ask me to sing. All the while, Marilyn silently assured me that I could go on. She told me that I would live through the upcoming Christmas holiday. I would most likely be walking around like a disjointed figure in a Picasso painting, but I would survive. I didn't understand the depth of her wisdom or the origin of her assurance until the evening she sent me home with a gift of a blue-glazed tea cup fresh from her kiln. As I cupped its rounded bottom in my hands and ran my lips across its rim, the din and anguish unexpectedly parted. A question floated before me in midair: *If lumps of clay and tree ash can transform into something else of beauty and purpose, then what about you?* It was the most wildly radical and liberating thought I had entertained in my life. It stopped me in my tracks as I crossed the drive separating our houses. What about me? Could I become something—someone—completely different? Someone new? Was I being transformed into someone other than who I had been? Was this the way of all life? I was suddenly standing in the middle of an unmown field of wildflowers all nodding their heads in unison: YES. At that moment I understood that life is a much larger dynamic than I ever dreamed possible. And that it was just waiting to introduce itself to me.

I am surprised to discover how intuitive my 16-year-old self is, how astute. She reminds me that my sixteenth year wasn't all bad, despite its trauma. There was also the small matter of selling my very first story to a nationally renowned newspaper. She, like the child me, thinks I haven't changed all that much over the years. Wasn't my first published piece a child's story about a girl who plants an apple seed in the earth only to be rewarded with a tree full of apples? She tells me that I have always loved Mother Earth and the mutually beneficial, symbiotic, intertwining relationships of all her creatures and inhabitants. She also tells me how brave, how courageous, I was when I was her, and that I must remember and reclaim this for myself going forward. She insists she has a lot to offer and admonishes me for giving her short-shrift.

What I am not surprised to discover is why I surround myself with Marilyn's pottery, which—after 45 years—threatens to overrun my kitchen, not to mention my shed. I can't decide if the transformed tree ash and clay is what holds the power, or the fact that the pottery is imprinted with Marilyn's hands, or because I can still hear the question—what I have since come to call the in-breaking of the Holy Spirit—parting the din and anguish of my 16-year-old self in order to be heard. In any case, I intentionally surround myself with Marilyn's teapots, bowls, plates, cups, and enchanting little vases, all of which emanate a subtle energy and vibrancy. It's no wonder that her magnificent glazed owl platter hangs in a place of honor inside The Bird's Nest.

In between visits from former selves, I am offered a reprieve of sorts. It comes in the shape of a dream, wherein I am visited by saints. It is a remarkable dream destined to be recorded in the leather-bound journal Frank bought for me at the base of the Rialto Bridge. It is a dream that crosses boundaries from the unconscious to the conscious, becoming an important reference point no matter what world I inhabit, no matter which iteration of me I am. Inside this dream world, I learn that all human beings are born with a silver thread growing from the crown of their heads—a thread, I am to understand, that connects them to the divine. The dream is an instruction, a lesson of sorts, though I am not sitting in a classroom. I don't appear to be anywhere recognizable. But that doesn't matter. What matters is that I am to remember that the silver string is my primary source of love. In my dream, I am asked: *Why demand and expect so much of others—not to mention yourself—when the source of what you need and want is as close as the crown of your head?* I don't know who is posing the question or what to say in response. So I listen—intently.

I am to know that all love and identity flow from the silver thread into me. More than that, I am to understand that people who forget—or, worse, don't know—about their own silver thread do the most damage to the world. The dream is all the more memorable for the fact that it comes to me during the eve of All Saints Day, a holy day of obligation I haven't celebrated since I was a child in Catholic grammar school. I awake with the knowledge that, for me, saints are the ones who knit the shimmery threads of love together into unified creation.

As difficult as the visit from my 16-year-old self is, the most challenging visitor just may be my 28-year-old-self. Though she also insists on revisiting unwanted memories, she, like my 16-year-old self, does not come without gifts. She reminds me how important it is not to be so invested in how I *want* life to be, that it's important to accept and work with what comes, to make a certain amount of allowances for fears and frailties—my own as well as others'. She presents memories of another major turmoil—one intimately connected to my life 12 years earlier when our mother's premature death had cast Sally and me as the "women of the house," when we finished raising ourselves through our turbulent teen years, mothered our younger brother, and became substitutes for anything in our household that required some semblance of womanly wherewithal. When I was 28, I suffered the demise of the fantasy that my family would be able to regroup into a cohesive, workable unit, along with the idea that I would be the one to make that happen. The fantasy I secretly nurtured had been a hope, a hidden assumption that I had carried through high school and college and into Frank's and my early marriage, until the day I realized what a fallacy it was. In the fullness of my 28th year, I finally acknowledged my own delusion. That's when I discovered that the death of a cherished idea—even one not consciously acknowledged—can be as devastating and as difficult to accommodate as any other death. My 28-year-old self wants me to remember and reclaim this truth in my newly evolving life. She wants me to be more realistic and truthful in my assessment of life. She reminds me that as much as I may have intended to cut myself off from the idea of religious faith, this cutting off is a complicated task—and not one to be taken lightly. She reminds me of how I was guided forward into a life-affirming story I could claim as my own. She reminds me of why I believe in miracles.

Just listen, Mark said gently, eyeing me with a mixture of compassion and concern as I grasped at some measure of composure through ragged tears. Just listen. Then, without introduction or explanation of any sort, he began reading aloud from a well-worn Bible he had pulled from the top drawer of his desk. In the next half hour, blind men were restored to sight, paralyzed men arose and walked, a young girl was resuscitated from her deathbed, and the menstrual flow of an anemic, emaciated, and outcast woman ceased—all because they had come into contact with Jesus. I may have been listening as Mark instructed, but I could not imagine what any of these ancient healings occurring at the behest of a man who walked the earth 2,000 years ago had to do with me. And, though real enough, my ailments were not physical. My problems were maddeningly invisible, stuffed way down inside the spiritual wasteland I inhabited, where they were growing increasingly restless and problematic and destructive by the day. "Daughter," Mark locked eyes with me as he finished reading the story of the resuscitated girl and the bleeding woman healed of her affliction, "be of good comfort. Thy faith hath made thee whole."

I sat there, stunned and silent. Had Jesus just called a woman daughter? In the same scripture passage in which Jesus restores Jairus' 12-year-old daughter to life, he heals a grown woman of incessant menstrual bleeding and addresses her as daughter! *Daughter!* The word hovered and shimmered in the air between us. Mark's sparse little office grew deeply quiet. It felt as if someone were reaching across the dry bones of the wilderness and speaking directly into my ear. *Whole.* These women—these daughters—weren't just healed, these daughters were made whole. Mark looked at me kindly as I careened around inside my head. "You shall know the truth and the truth shall make you free," he said.

I cast my eye across the entire debacle of my mother's death and ensuing fracturing of my family, and could not find words to articulate the toll all of it had taken on what had been an infantile, unworkable faith in the face of crisis. I had come of age in a church that conveyed condescension toward and distrust of females (beyond the Virgin Mary, of course), a church that considered women so "unclean" that newborns were presented to the priest for baptism by anyone but the baby's mother because she was in all likelihood bleeding following childbirth. Yet, here were stories in the Bible that spoke lovingly and compassionately about women. Here was Jairus, the father of the young woman on her deathbed, pleading and crying for Jesus to save his daughter's life. And here was Jesus, so clearly unafraid of bleeding women, so clearly moved to compassion in light of the ill woman's suffering that he staunches the blood flow. With the death of my mother and disintegrated relationship with my father, at age 28 it was made clear to me that my sense of "daughterhood" lay in tatters. It took me a full minute before I could speak. "I'm afraid there is no truth," I said. This was certainly apostasy. And if not apostasy, it was surely blasphemy. I was going to hell, if, that is, I wasn't already there.

"Oh, but there is," Mark assured me. "And you know enough that you were able to come in here today looking for it."

I shook my head, genuinely perplexed, as I glanced around to get my bearings. "I was just walking by on my way to the post office. Someone else must have opened the door. Honestly, I don't even know what a Christian Science Reading Room is."

"Well, you do now." Mark smiled and reached out to shake my hand. "It's an honor to meet you," he said, handing me his card and a Bible to take home. "Your healing has already begun. Call me anytime. Transformations can be messy. You can be caught off guard."

"No kidding," I said, not completely understanding what he meant, but catching the barest crack of hope shining under the door anyway.

Given that I hadn't even known I was in need of healing, no one was more surprised by my encounter with a Christian Science practitioner than I. I made it my mission to read the entire Bible Mark had given me—not only the stories of Jesus in the *New Testament*, but the majorly confusing and mind-bending epic histories chronicled in the *Old Testament* as well. That's where I unexpectedly discovered the beauty and assurance of the Psalms, particularly Psalm 116 and Psalm 138, which share a similar sentiment: "On the day I called, you answered me. You increased my strength of soul." To my 28-year-old self-caught in an unending loop of unresolved resentment and fury, the Psalms were a balm, words so potent that taken together they formed an antidote to despair. Even so, my way up and out of the old disastrous assumptions I had embraced at my mother's grave was not a straight, triumphant trajectory. It was always two steps forward and one back; it was a lot of rallying and failing and flailing about, with me sometimes sliding back full throttle into the crevasse of despair. One question answered opened up 10 more that weren't. But Mark was always there on the other end of the telephone, just waiting, it seemed, for me to call with questions,

\\sions, and outright incredulity regarding the claims of the Christian story.

It was my 28-year-old self who finally developed the "strength of soul" to look back across the previous 12 years of spiritual alienation to recognize how blinded I had been by fury and grief and arrogance. It was my 28-year-old self who was finally able to grasp life's underlying dynamic of resurrection playing out in untold ways across the crucible of creation. Like the tattooed sales associate at the mega home improvement store, if I had had a propensity for marking my body with personally significant biblical passages, at age 28 I would have tattooed "Psalm 138" or "Psalm 116" on my arms, along with three other scriptural references: Matthew 9:18-25, Mark 5:22-42, and Luke 8:41-56. All three recount the story of the intertwining healings of the daughter at death's door and the older woman suffering from a particularly female affliction who Jesus addresses as "daughter." Through the medium of story, both women reached across time and space, encouraging me to reach out and touch the hem of Jesus' dusty cloak. I never, not in a million years, had imagined that an ancient story shrouded in old-fashioned English could open the door to liberation and salvation.

Despite my dramatic transition from a tattered faith life into a more mature assessment of the divine, I remain skeptical of organized religion. And despite entering graduate school to study theology with the Jesuits, I remain skittish about committing to any one worship community or embracing any one absolute definition of God. I cannot join a group that insists that the divine must fit into a set of prescribed rituals and creeds. For me, God feels too big, too expansive, to accommodate any humanly imposed limits, though if I had to choose one particular understanding of God as expressed within the church it is that of the Jesuits. Officially known as the Society of Jesus and founded in the 16th century by Saint Ignatius, Jesuits engage in relationship with the divine through the act of emotional discernment and personal imagination in prayer. Jesuits believe God is constantly laboring in the details and detritus of our lives to liberate us from erroneous assumptions and destructive attitudes and behaviors that prevent us from learning to love ourselves and others. Jesuits ask: *How can your life be lived to its greatest good? How can love be best enacted in whatever situation you find yourself?* Their answer always lies in the very real and interactive process of sifting, mining, and refining individual personal experience in light of the greater good. There are many ways of living a good life; it is the *magis*, or greatest good for our individual lives, that Jesuits are always striving for. Human life working in tandem with the divine is at the core of their faith. Paying attention to daily life is the stuff of eternal life.

Praying what is known as the *Daily Examen* at the close of every day is at the heart of their spiritual practice. As practical an approach to prayer as I could ever hope to find, the *Daily Examen* is an exercise consisting of five elements: (1) Begin by praying for light, illumination, graced understanding. (2) Move into reviewing the day with thanksgiving and gratitude, from hour to hour, place to place, task to task; include a review of dreams. (3) Conduct a feelings review of the day; emotions indicate the liveliest index of what is happening in our lives and point to underlying truths or problems to be worked out. (4) Then, focus on one feeling that most catches your attention. Pray from it; it is a sign that something important is going on. Attend to the source of that feeling. (5) End by looking forward into the morrow to see what feelings surface. Whatever those feelings are, turn them into prayer. For me, this approach to developing an interactive relationship between human and divine is pure genius. How else are we to discover the macrocosm of existence except by looking to the microcosm of our lives?

Mostly, I go to church in the river bottoms. I pray alongside beaver lodges and footbridges of the Rockery—those magnificent boulders hefted into tunnels and trails alongside the Audubon sanctuary's pond. I rejoice in the feel of walking along dirt roads and trails at Appleton Farms. It is both spiritual and physical, this feeling that comes over me as I go out into the land. It is a rich resonance, a silent sound. And it wakes me in the middle of the night—a shaft of moonlight to my breast bone—nudging me to get up, to look out the window at the moon casting its white diamond light across the snow, making me sit up and gently touch the indentation of the back of Frank's neck as he sleeps beside me, prodding me along the darkened hallway toward Bethany's and Tyler's now empty bedrooms where I rejoice in vestiges of their childhood and delight in their new-found adulthoods, amazed that I, among all women, have been the conduit for their lives. The throbbing awareness of being so connected, so *resurrected*, demands my full attention. It heals. It aches. It overwhelms. I tiptoe downstairs to connect match to wick and get lost in candle flame. I cannot contain this love of all things, this enveloping beauty. It is in me and it is everywhere.

Following her difficult early years, Beatrix Potter found what her biographer Margaret Lane calls the "deliciousness of life" as a mature woman. Her farms, her sheepdogs, her country village life in the early 1900s—Beatrix Potter loved all of it. And her artistry! How wonderful was that to be a financially successful, independent artist and author in a time and place and culture so arrogantly dismissive of women's talents and sense of self? She gloried in her later life in the English Lake District. As Lane writes: "...she had expressed her sense of the deliciousness of her life there—her delight in the old house with its attics and cupboards, in the farmyard, the stone-walled pastures surrounding it, the woods and foxgloves, the lad's love and the lilies in the little front garden of Sawrey, the aroma of bacon and groceries in the village shop." What a gift to be not just content, but *enchanted*, with life. As I write about Beatrix Potter inside my shed, I think about what Lane calls Beatrix Potter's "invisible thread of sympathy" with the small creatures she painted, not to mention the whole of creation. She could not contain this love of all things, this enveloping beauty. It was in her, and it was everywhere.

Chapter 12

"Ravine Syndrome" or the Sacred Swamp

Despite its obviously manufactured ambiance, I am enthralled with the trendy retailer Anthropologie. Its marketing strategy invites consumers to create a new vision for their lives the minute they step through the door of their brick-and-mortar stores. That's why it is on my list of "artist outing" destinations, which writer and creative guru Julia Cameron recommends as an essential part of life for all 'creatives.' Her books and workshops require participants to, among other things, take themselves on what she calls "an artist date," an outing of color, inspiration, and idea enrichment on a weekly basis. Anthropologie is not exactly the

Boston Museum of Fine Arts or the Symphony, but it serves the purpose—my purpose, anyway—very well. I can't resist the store's charms. It is part art gallery, time capsule, playroom, clothing store, houseware emporium, book shop, and apothecary of intriguing perfumes and bath products. And, the store's background music is not 'muzak,' of course, but something folksy and sprightly and spunky, a musical playlist upbeat enough to get me humming along. Seemingly disconnected objects (books stacked on the same table as glittery necklaces, ceramic tea cups, and hand lotions) are displayed alongside one another, with color seeming to be the organizing principle. Its inventory encourages artistry, experimentation, and the adventure of identifying and creating new and unexpected relationships.

Although the store's inventory is pricey, and I tend to be a tightwad, during my last visit to Anthropologie in Harvard Square, I almost bought *The Forest Feast*—a cook book (of sorts) that includes the story of the author's journey from New York's concrete canyons to California's redwoods. The book includes intriguing photos of farm-fresh, candlelight dinners on the author's deck overlooking a lush forest. It speaks of adventure, new possibilities, color, and atmosphere. For a woman evolving into a new iteration of herself, this book has certain appeal. I managed to corral my common sense just seconds before approaching the cashier with book in hand. I was awash in daydreams of entertaining new scintillating and urbane friends on my own back deck overlooking the ravine when I suddenly remembered that I don't like to cook.

The only time I'll step foot into a shopping mall in December is during off-hours, when it is less crammed with frenzied Christmas shoppers than usual, and even then that is enough to try my soul. Just the opening *whoosh* of the heavy glass doors and that first scent of stale popcorn from the mall cinema wafting down linoleum hallways rocks me back on my heels. The giant fake tinseled Christmas trees and the 'muzak' version of "The Little Drummer Boy" piped over the sound system set my teeth on edge. As I pass by several puppies lolling aimlessly around in wood chips in the pet store's window, I am completely dispirited. On the way home from the mall, I stop in Bradley Palmer State Park, where I walk along the Ipswich River in solitude among birches arching across a swirling current. I spy a semi-submerged beaver lodge—a great hump of sticks and mud out among the marshes. I am already feeling more buoyant. As dusk falls, I find my way home and into my shed, where I write by the glow of a red Coleman lantern and bid the trees and beavers and creatures of the ravine good night.

Overnight, snow begins to fall. It falls all the next day, sifting through the trees in the ravine, which at this time of year resemble gray vertical bones. It is so gray. Amazingly enough, despite the frost and freezing temperatures, the rosemary plants in the pots outside The Bird's Nest are flourishing, still pungent with scent when I take off my gloves and run my hands up their soft, limber stems. I drive up to Marini Farm, which at Christmastime is transformed into a pine-scented yuletide wonderland. The big old barn that offers me respite from the summer heat is now stuffed to the rafters with pine boughs, evergreens, wreaths, tubs of ornaments, and twinkling lights. I buy a 10-inch balsam wreath and bring it home to hang on the door of my shed. But first, I affix the wreath with a bright-red bow and the carved wooden face of a gnome that I have saved from Christmas to Christmas for years.

It's been weeks since I have spotted any deer, though their tracks are in the muddy snow in the front of my shed. Clearly, they have come to call when I was not at home. I am wondering if word has gone out amid the underbrush that I inadvertently hit a beaver as I drove home in the dark along one of Topsfield's back roads. The pelted animal had looked so purposeful, so earnest, its eyes a flash of brilliance at the edge of the marsh as it blundered into traffic. The last thing I wanted to do a week before Christmas was to kill a forest creature. As a gesture of contrition and reconciliation, I place our enormous leftover Halloween pumpkin on the edge of the ravine for the creatures to have their own forest feast. I awake the next morning to find that the pumpkin has been shredded down to its base. Even its stem is gone. Racoons? Fox? Groundhogs? Maybe there was a party. I am hoping I am forgiven for trespassing in untold ways into the animal world.

At zero degree Fahrenheit, it only makes sense to remain in the house in front of a fire. I can't even think about heading out to my shed on its frigid hillside. As I get ready for bed, a brilliant full moon rises. Its luminous presence follows me around the house from room to room. It hangs in the sky, ready to spill its light across the back yard once it ascends the roofline of our house. I know the moon is there while I run a bath, brush my teeth, and pull back the bed covers. I dart from window to window to check its progress in the sky. I feel sure forest creatures are basking in its liquid light, though it's actually more likely that they are hiding in the shadows, either waiting to pounce or seeking concealment depending upon their position in the food chain. I fall asleep to the sound of brittle tree branches cracking and creaking in the wind as prescient words of Thoreau arise like a puff of smoke from the nether reaches of my mind: *"God culminates in the present moment."*

I go on a milk run to Appleton Farms Dairy Store in Ipswich, which is not at all like a milk run into Cumberland Farms in downtown Topsfield. At "Cumby's," the minute I dash into the store, I am assailed by the smell of coffee and harsh glow of fluorescent lighting. Its check-out counter is crowded with rolls of lottery tickets secured behind thick transparent partitions, cartons of cigarettes, chewing gum, candy bars and—at Christmas—candy canes or red-nosed reindeer lapel pins. It's the typical convenience store. When it comes to Appleton Farms, there's no dashing to be done. It emanates what I can only call the elusive quality of soul. To reach its door, I must drive up a long dirt and gravel road bisecting farm fields and low-slung stone walls. At this time of year, the fields resemble the Arctic tundra. The car tires crunch and squeak along fresh snowfall atop frozen dirt. In summer, the farm's community supported agriculture members collect their weekly produce allotment inside the store's adjacent antique barn, which on summer evenings is transformed with sparkly white lights and wooden picnic tables for communal potluck suppers. Since the store opens directly into the barn, the entire building during the summer is imbued with the effervescence of fresh vegetables—zucchini, cucumbers, carrots, tomatoes, and potatoes. But in winter, the barn is empty and closed off, and its adjacent little store is downright frigid. I pause, if only for a moment, under its beams to take in the rough texture of the wide pine boards beneath my boots, its muted lighting, its earthy scent of gnarly sweet potatoes, still dusted with last summer's dirt, tumbling from an old washtub on the floor.

The cashier is huddled in her coat and colorful knitted hat behind the wooden counter. Despite the chill, I linger inside this place and chat with the saleswoman. I take my time exchanging the thick-glassed empty milk bottles I brought back to the store for bottles full of fresh milk from cows that live just a stone's throw up the dirt road. At the checkout counter, I sample a new cheese product made from their milk and decide to buy a wedge. Its buttery, nutty flavor will be delicious with Kalamata olives. At the last minute, I see a small jar of locally produced pesto, and buy that, too, along with a small paper bag of English Rose Tea—a blend made in Ipswich from English Breakfast tea and beach roses that grow up and down the North Shore. I suddenly realize that I can't leave without buying the last loaf of artisan baguette as well. It will be perfect with the pesto. I succumb to the spell of the small store, which in modern America is about as inconvenient as it could possibly be—something I find irresistibly charming. On the way out the door, I stop to read a birth announcement tacked up on the wallboards: Enid, Salt, Rosebud, Myra, and Mercy are now sharing the world with us. Their adorable little Jersey faces—square noses, moist nostrils, and huge liquid brown eyes—are inquisitive, docile, curious. They gaze directly at the photographer who has zeroed in for a close-up. Woolen coats are buckled around their small calf chests. I am enchanted by their mini bovine wardrobe, intrigued by the fact that little cows need clothes.

There are not many one-of-a-kind authentic shops still operating in this country—a fact that I, and others like me, bemoan. Everything is scaled for efficiency, for maximizing profits, for creating a uniformity of reliable consumer experience. Chain stores reign supreme. In reading an article recently about a much-loved businessman from Boston's South Shore who operated a vintage household variety store for decades, I am astonished by an admission he made to the reporter. On the eve of his store's closing, the reporter had asked the man if he had had any regrets. The businessman confessed that, yes, he had suffered great regret in the 1950s after he had allowed a linoleum salesman to talk him into jackhammering a spectacular slab of Italian marble from the store's old-fashioned soda fountain and replacing it with linoleum countertop. Fifty years after the fact, the desecration was still a source of regret.

I can think 'spring' all I want, but it turns out that we are in between major snowstorms. Every weekend for the past four weeks, storms have marched across the region and dumped a solid 18 to 24 inches of snow. It's like clockwork. Meanwhile, The Bird's Nest has transformed into an igloo. Despite the fact that it's frigid inside its four walls, I continue to dig a path out to it and try to spend at least 15 minutes writing at my desk. I gaze out the double window facing the ravine and am surprised to see a tiny, yet hardy, songbird winging its way through bare trees. Following one of the storms, a bird landed at our dining room window and sang out earnestly after tucking a small husk of dried grass in between the window casing and surrounding frame. I'm sure it is longing for spring, just like the rest of us. I'm assuming it will be back for its treasure at some point. Beyond these tiny birds, there are not many other animal sightings. There are no animal tracks in the new snow at all when I go out to shovel a path to my shed yet again. I look up to the roof of the garage to see an enormous snow wave, frozen in mid-crest, arched along the edge of the front gutter line.

When I step out onto our back deck, the boards beneath my feet crack and boom, contracting sharply in these single-digit temperatures. They are so loud that they startle a red-tailed hawk perched in a bare branch high above my head. The air is so cold it feels like glass. I look down at the path I have shoveled from the back deck to the steps leading up into The Bird's Nest and see fresh rabbit tracks. The rabbit that lives beneath the deck near the hot tub climbed up and out of its burrow in the night, traversed an enormous snow bank, and landed in the middle of the path. It left tracks all the way down the path to the shed, then up and over another mountain of snow before scooting under The Bird's Nest. I am glad to be of service to the comings and goings of cottontails. Anyone who has a rabbit as a totem is identified as sensitive and artistic. According to Jane's reference book, rabbits also represent fertility and new life. I still can't figure out how and when an animal actually becomes a person's totem, but I like the possibilities inherent in all those that appear to be mine—groundhog, robin, and rabbit. Every last one seems to be escorting me into a new life.

One person's sacred text is another's dense and dull tome. So it is with Herman Melville's *Moby-Dick*. In my mind, it's about as dense and dull a book as I can imagine. Nevertheless, I accompany Frank on a spur-of-the-moment day-trip to New Bedford one weekend in an attempt to investigate an unknown destination and escape the tedium of snow-blowing and shoveling out the driveway once again. Unknown to us, hundreds of other people had the same idea to travel to the port of origin of Melville's whaling classic. On arrival in the historic center of the city, we discover that New Bedford is celebrating Melville's birthday with a 24-hour public reading of *Moby-Dick*. With heads bent over books as well as Kindles, Nooks and other e-readers, Melville devotees jammed the New Bedford Whaling Museum's large foyer as they followed along with a reader at a microphone set up in the middle of the hall. It was astounding to see the number of people who had not only set aside an entire weekend to attend a public reading but who had also stayed up all night in order to do so—and for a book I could never finish, let alone begin. In several attempts to read the book, I never got much beyond "Call me Ishmael." As the reader in the museum turned to the book's final page, people rose to their feet in adulation, applauded, high-fived, stamped their feet, cat-called, whistled, and wept. I watched, transfixed, as the power of story swept across a tribe of people celebrating its sacred text.

Despite my admiration for Willa Cather and my love of her novels, they do not quite occupy sacred text status in my mind. That exalted position belongs to Alice Walker's *The Color Purple* and Eudora Welty's *The Optimist's Daughter*, both of which I encountered in my twenties. I came upon the books shelved side-by-side in a basement bookstore in Harvard Square. Something about their subject matter suggested that they were part and parcel of the same story, part and parcel of my story. That they were shelved side-by-side just clinched the deal. I devoured them both in the same weekend. If it's possible to love a literary figure, I loved Celie in *The Color Purple* from the book's opening line. Celie writes letters to God in search of help and answers. Her greatest strength is that she believes God is listening, despite having encountered much evidence in life to the contrary. Unlike me, she does not succumb to apostasy. Then there's Laurel in *The Optimist's Daughter*, who realizes on the last page of the book that the memory of her dead mother does not live in the bread board her mother had used to fashion her signature loaves of bread, but in freedom and forgiveness that make all things new. Despite the fact that Celie and Laurel are fictional characters, both share "spirit sister" status with a few of my select living, breathing friends.

It's the end of March, officially spring, and a light fairy snow is sifting from the skies—one to three inches expected. On a walk to the old stone bridge on Perkins Row, I look up to see a "snow ghost," which is nothing more than crystals sifting off pine trees and glinting and swirling in the sun before disappearing. Despite this unexpected brilliant snow, the winter wearies have made an encore. I stop by the Topsfield Library as a diversion, and discover that it is stocking an heirloom seed library. Patrons can share seed packets of peas, beans, beets, carrots, lettuce, tomatoes, and dill. If our yard had a shred of sunshine, I would be tempted to take some home. I am heartened just by the imaginative display of the seed envelopes filed alphabetically inside narrow wooden drawers of an antique card catalogue case. Just to think of anything green and growing is a tonic when it's 15 degrees Fahrenheit outside. No wonder farming families in days of yore spent long, dark winters poring over seed catalogues. Instead of succumbing to the allure of seeds that I can't use, I decide to order trim Capri cotton pants and a pair of ballet flats from the Lands End catalogue waiting for me in the mailbox when I arrive home.

Some days require a little more stamina than others, especially if a good night's sleep has gone by the boards the night before. On a day when I feel particularly stretched thin, I push my way through chores and freelance job responsibilities until late afternoon, when I give it all up and head down to the stone bridge along Perkins Row. Despite the snow-covered marshes, several Canada geese are floating along thin streams cutting through the frozen landscape. The geese set up a din as I make my way down the embankment. They are not happy with me. Nor are they happy with a mallard and his mate swimming nearby and hopping on and off ice ledges. Despite what they feel about me, I am ecstatic to see them. It is also restorative to look up in the trees and see chickadees and red-winged blackbirds trilling above my head. And then—there it is—the great blue heron. It was lurking in the shallows until it revealed itself by pumping its wide wings across the marshes to alight in a faraway tree. Such ungainly grace! Such a long stretch of neck! Such knobby knees and sticks for legs! I never dreamed I would see my old friend now—today—in this winter that just won't go away. On my walk home, I pick up a lovely scroll of white birch bark freshly shed from the side of a tree. It's like paper. I could write a poem on it. I think of the words I wrote with Sharpie on the last piece of exposed insulation in The Bird's Nest before paneling over it: *"I went to the marsh at twilight, to see the great blue heron that lives there…"* Once inside my shed, I write the phrase all over again on my new-found birch bark and watercolor a delicate great blue heron as illustration. I affix it to the pine paneling just beneath the awning window and patiently wait for spring.

Finally! The peepers are tuning up their high-pitched chorus. Something down deep in the ravine begins "glump, glump, glump"—as if a grumpy old man were at the bottom of a well. And then, there strikes up a trilling, a peeping cast of thousands. The air is vibrating with sound swarming up from below and surrounding my shed. I am suddenly encased in wild ecstatic soundwaves. The heartbeat of the universe pulsates in the throatings of tiny brown and green frogs. Just being alive here with them is sacrament. This is the day that turns out to be the pivotal day, the hinge between winter and spring—55 degrees and sunny. It's time to prepare my shed for real usage again, not just five or 10 minutes of cramped-finger writing in sub-zero temperatures. I sweep out the floor, clear away cobwebs, wipe down shelving, and re-hang Sally's framed needle-work sampler on the back wall next to Marilyn's owl platter.

Oh, the slant of the sun is perfect, so long now, extending its reach into the ravine and across the roofline of my shed. I rake out my shade garden and find sprouts coming up between what appear to be dead sticks, remainders of last year's plants. I walk up the rise and inspect the tiny, sharp reddish buds of the crab apple. She and I have a heart-to-heart. I remind her of all the plant meal I spread around the base of her trunk last fall. I tell her that it's important for the universe that she blossom, that she become what she is meant to be. The same could be said for me.

Right here, right now, it's magic. The peepers and frogs of the ravine are making a cacophony! I am thrilled to hear the wild, crazy song of ecstasy they are chorusing into the evening air. There is absolute amazement in the presence of the NOW. In the middle of the night, I awake to hear them loud and clear through our open bedroom window. Suddenly, all at once, as if the choral director has indicated *pianissimo*, they quiet down *en masse*. But they are incorrigible, uncontrollable. After a minute of a low-level humming, they are up and at it again full throttle. They are enraptured by being alive!

On my days off from work, I have a hard time choosing between going out to my writing shed to write with pen in lined notebooks or spending time editing and transcribing my notes into my resulting manuscript on the computer. I feel I am hitting my stride in transitioning words from pen to computer, so I choose to be indoors doing that rather than outside in my sanctuary. The curious thing is that when I choose one thing, I long to be doing the other. It's maddening.

No matter where I am in my endeavor to process and record thoughts on the lip of this land, I wonder and worry about the life of the wetlands in the ravine. I'm not alone in my concern. The Massachusetts Audubon Society is studying the effects of climate change on this ecosystem. So many creatures rely on the temporary nature of vernal ponds; they depend on a balance of precipitation and evaporation in order to survive. Too much water, and a vernal pond will become consistently wet enough to support fish— disastrous for the lower life forms that would then become fish food. Too shallow or dried up altogether, and vernal pond organisms may not have enough time to complete their developmental stages. Either way, it's endangerment or, perhaps, extinction. A vernal pond's temporary nature is what makes it the ideal platform for certain life forms to flourish. Transitory organisms flourish in a transitory environment. They all have a part to play in this massive, groaning, unfolding universe, as, I believe, do I—as transitory as I may be.

I often think on the fact that I did not arrive on earth by my own volition. I did not will myself into being. When I think of the interplay of temperature, minerals, elements, genetic linking, chemical actions and reactions that have created and continue to create conditions within this unfolding universe that optimizes life— my life—on this planet, I can barely breathe. It is too overwhelming to contemplate.

It amazes me daily how long we lived in this house, on this land adjacent to the ravine, without me being remotely conscious of its throbbing presence. Now, several years after my encounter with a patch of lichen clinging to a tree, watching fiddlehead ferns unfurl is a show unto itself. Gently and deliberately, they raise their chins and stretch their necks up and back, tilting their feathered leaves upward. I look up into the branches of Miss Crab Apple and am convinced that she is flowering. Small white clusters of blossoms edged with pink tips are spreading along slender branches. It's a momentous day! The foliage of the forest is creating its summer canopy where birds and other wild ones can conceal themselves. Paper wasps are once again constructing a nest under the overhang of my shed. Talk about purposeful intent! I watch them fly in under the overhang, construct tiny, six-sided compartments that all connect together perfectly, and then fly off again. It takes an enormous amount of energy and time to build a shelter that can be so easily destroyed. So much effort is invested in being alive.

Such, fresh, cool air! So fresh and cool, in fact, that Frank and I stroll down to the old stone bridge along Perkins Row at twilight. First, I look back to what I call "the past"—over the left side of the bridge to a well-defined demarcation of trees at that end of the marsh—and then I look to "the future"—that area of the waterway that curves up around a bend into the un-seeable, the land that appears to be without limits. The stone bridge spanning the watery marsh grasses and ponds where I stand is "the present." I am participating in what I call "deep time," or "trinity time," when I am conscious that the past, present, and future ignite simultaneously. As Frank and I hold hands and stroll toward home, I recite a mantra that arrives out of nowhere: *We live in a beautiful house, in a beautiful place, along the edge of a ravine, in a beautiful space.*

There are times when I wonder if I have a case of "ravine syndrome," akin to what occurs to those who visit the holy sites of Jerusalem. I have read that it is not uncommon for Christian pilgrims to be physically and emotionally overcome while walking in the footsteps of Jesus in old Jerusalem. They cannot continue. They fall to the ground. With their receptivity to the divine on overdrive, they succumb. They appear to fall into a psychotic state, or trance. They believe they have seen the face of God on *Via Dolorosa*. It's known as "Jerusalem Syndrome."

I have never been to Jerusalem, but here on the edge of the ravine, I can easily fall into a suspended state, a type of trance. I sense that something sacred moves among the trees and scuffs the surface of the pond. The ground creatures are privy to its message, so when they make their way up to our grassy clearing from the bottom of the ravine and poke their heads through the underbrush, I feel that they have something to say, that they may be messengers of sorts. The animals' presence feels portentous. This feeling must be the origin of the idea of animal totems. Native American beliefs reflect this awareness of hidden, underlying presence. Indigenous peoples' sacred grounds—nothing more than ordinary hills, buttes, and mountains to the uninitiated—are believed to be more than the sum of soil deposits, the residue of glaciers, or long-ago seismic activity. In a similar vein, Celtic Christian spirituality makes room for the idea that certain geographic formations especially vibrate with the divine energy embedded in all creation. Called "thin places," it is believed that God is more easily apprehended at those locations than at others. So it is for me at the edge of the ravine.

Wet. Wet. Wet. Much needed rain is pelting my writing shed and dripping down its screens. I suppose the frogs are loving this. After the recent drought, I know the plants are. In any event, it is verdant. It is a green so green it is luminescent. Every green living, breathing leaf is vibrating green. It is Hildegard von Bingen green. I think the color of gratitude, not envy, must be green. If the process of photosynthesis manifests in the world as a color, it is this lush, radiant green. At this time of year, rhododendrons are out and making a scene, but they are not just green. They are bursting with buds the same color as my new summer sandals—a deep, rich fuchsia.

To reach my shed in the back, I decide to make a detour out the front door, down the porch steps and out along the drive, and circumnavigate the house just so I can spend time with the rhododendrons rioting along our drive. I am greeted inside The Bird's Nest by a slice of sun illuminating the wood-grain of my desk, as a large bee buzzes drowsily around the window screens. *"Can I come in?"* it asks. I look down at my unfinished manuscript and wonder if I will ever finish, if anything at all will come of all the jottings and writings and drawings. The frogs and the birds and other creatures of pond and forest tell me that I don't have to accomplish anything of great magnitude in this life. I ask myself what could I possibly hope to accomplish that would make any difference in this complex, unfolding interweaving of worlds. Under the exposed wooden beams of The Bird's Nest, I let go of the notion that I must account for, or justify, my existence. I can just be me—a poet passing through—if that's all I want to be. I am who I am. And, like every other living organism in creation, every day I am living into the dying of me. I watch birds—twigs in beaks—dive and dart across the back clearing, observe squirrels and chipmunks collect acorns and nuts, inspect spiders spinning webs, and watch dragonflies whirring about on their window-pane wings. All of these creatures perform the task they are endowed to do. They live in the minutiae of the moment while the larger forces of the universe grind on. I take their lessons to heart and decide to sweep out my shed.

Summer weekends evaporate. There is too much to do, and too little time to do it in. This weekend (as every summer weekend), Frank is impatient to be out and away on The Flying Dutchman. He doesn't want to spend time mowing the lawn or trimming bushes or clearing a plugged drain. Who can blame him? He decides to release himself from chores and head to the yacht club. I, on the other hand, head out on a bike ride, stopping to talk to plants that clearly have no other purpose than to delight in the day: A field of purple lupines poking their heads up among wild grasses, black-eyed-susans behind a break of pines, an embankment of ferns rearing their heads back in laughter underneath an ancient oak in deep shade, a circle of stately yellow-throated purple irises leaning in toward one another to preen and chat in a formal garden at the end of a neighbor's drive. As lovely and colorful as the flowers are, the real gift of the day is the green heron that swoops in low across the Great Wenham Swamp and alights near me on the top of a semi-submerged beaver lodge. When I slow my bike to get a good look at its lustrous deep green feathers, it takes off into a nearby copse. I ride home to pull out my watercolors and paint the bird's crow-like body, its green and burgundy-brushed feathers. It couldn't look any different from the majestic blue heron if it tried, though there is a faint family resemblance in the hunched slump of its neck and shoulders.

I meet up with Frank at the yacht club during what I call "heaven's light," that time of late afternoon when the sun illuminates and blends sea and sky in a soft, pearly light. The boats' white hulls, which are all pointed out to sea by the trick of the tides, are numinous, as if surrounded by haloes. They appear to be pointing toward some cosmic answer: *There. Look there. You'll find all the answers to the universe out beyond that pink horizon.* Before I can ride the launch out to meet Frank on The Flying Dutchman, he is using the boat's two-way radio to call for the launch himself. The Flying Dutchman must remain in the harbor. There are small craft warnings for Salem Sound, says the robotic voice on the marine weather radio station broadcasting from the launch driver's shed. That's when I notice how turbulent the water is, how the boats are bucking up and down on the incoming waves, how their lines are suddenly taut one minute and slack the next. Waves roll up behind their sterns and slap their bottoms. Frank and I decide to take advantage of the turn in the weather to go home and settle in on the back porch for reading time and the luxury of a nap. At night, we head out for a soak in the hot tub. Two shooting stars—one right after the other—combust before our eyes in an inky, unsettled sky.

At 4:20 a.m., in the darkness outside our bedroom window, there's struggle. I sit straight up in bed when I hear a piercing, high-pitched scream echo across the ravine. Fear and pain is embedded in the sound. Distress. Death. Destruction. It seems to last for a good five minutes or more. It stops. Then, once again, full throttle. The scream is followed by a thunderous, furious flapping of wings. Then silence. My heart thumps in my chest. I pat the blankets next to me to wake Frank up, but suddenly remember that he is away on business. I wonder if our new neighbors across the ravine have heard the scream. The acoustics in this cool, clear night air are so fine-tuned that I have an auditory ringside seat on whatever is happening below in the dark. I feel sure it is a great, large owl on the hunt, that its razor-sharp beak and talons have invaded the home of a fairly large ground creature. I can't imagine a mouse screaming that loudly. There are, of course, all sorts of animals prowling around in the ravine and our back yard under cover of darkness. They knock over a pot of dirt on our back porch, leave their prints in the mud near my writing shed. They dislodge a tiny blue-glazed pot from a small pond tableau I have constructed of moss and twigs and a life-sized turtle figurine near my shed's steps. All the ground creatures are aware that my shed offers an undercover escape route into the ravine. I know The Bird's Nest receives visitors while I am away and enmeshed in dreams. It becomes a sanctuary of sorts for creatures other than me.

Scientists are seemingly not impressed by prolific species. There are so many birds and hedgerow plants to be labeled and identified, so many life forms. Is there any point in being amazed when one comes into view? And how to name them all? They become "common"—an appellation that never fails to offend me. I think "humble" would be a better qualifier. Listed in my *Kaufman Field Guide to the Nature of New England*, there's the common evening primrose, the common tansy, common milkweed, and common blue violet. I can vouch for the fact that there is nothing common about the sizeable woolly leaves of the common mullein—a tall stalk that bursts into Provence-yellow buds once it reaches full stature, which I would guess to be about three or four feet high. It's a sturdy sort, not overly fussy about where it sets down roots, its most favorable location being ditches and deserted roadways. There is something remarkable about being able to flourish anywhere—a true survival skill, if there ever was one, and evidence of strength of soul. An extraordinary specimen of this particular species is flourishing at the edge of our back clearing, just to the left of The Bird's Nest. I barely notice it until it bursts into bud. *Surprise!* It seems to say. *I may be common, but I'm outstandingly resilient!*

My friend Jeannie who lives along coastal New Hampshire tells me that she takes great pride in showing visitors the beauty of the shore's coastal cliffs, the area's quaint towns, bucolic farmlands, and river estuaries. I know what she means. There is something empowering about showing someone else the beauty of the world. There's something appropriately boastful about it, because we are not the ones who have created it. "Just look at that expanse!" I'll exclaim to a friend as we gaze out across Rockport's tiny harbor to the endless undulating ocean glinting in the sun. "Immanence."

There is the sweetest of bird sounds, the most golden, silk-like trill, coming from the ravine in early mornings now. I am wondering: Is it the mythic wood thrush that the early colonists remarked upon? Has the swamp angel come to call? Is this the mystery of the universe rising from the wetlands at the bottom of the ravine? How wonderful would it be to be a bird, to spread my feathers and fly out across the ravine? Since there is not the remotest chance of this happening, I decide to build a swing—one with a broad wooden seat that hangs suspended from a sturdy branch of an oak at the very edge of the ravine. I want to pump my legs and feel the rush of the wind as I fly out across the ferns and forested hillside, dissolving into the green of all green, and sing an ode to green:

Oh, I don't know anything,

Except that I love the color of green.

The color of green of the sun through the trees,

There's no more beautiful veil than these.

It is still.

So still.

The entire universe has settled down inside of me. There is not a breath of air blowing outside. It's a "three-H" day: Hot, humid, hazy. The leaves on the trees in the ravine are limp clumps of greenery, as if they are having a bad hair day. My mood matches the desultory feeling of the outdoors. Is it coincidence or synchronicity that I come upon this small saying from the 13th-century Turkish Sufi poet Rumi today?

Do not be lonely.

The entire universe

Is inside of you.

It is the season of tiny brown-speckled frogs so cute and cunning that I want to catch them in the palms of my hands and kiss their tiny heads. They "poing" through the underbrush, making blades of grass bend and move mysteriously on a day when there is not a breath of air anywhere. I look closely to find several leaping their way from the hydrangea bush to the day lilies. A green frog, a little larger than the tiny brown frogs, has backed itself into the curvature of a hydrangea leaf, looking exactly like a hydrangea leaf itself. Such a superior case of camouflage. I watch a brown frog the size of my fingernail propel itself off the porch and soar the length of a nine-foot arc above my head to land somewhere in the grass at my feet. Its aerial high jinks snap me out of my heat stupor. I perk up in amazement. If some part of that frog dwells inside the entire universe that dwells inside of me, then I am beyond content. I am buoyant with happiness.

I am inspired by the Canadian painter Emily Carr, who did not come into the fullness of herself until she was well into her fifth decade. She found herself, quite literally, in the great Pacific Northwest old-growth forests, where she slavishly reproduced the natural surroundings and totem poles of people of the First Nations. She had spent her youth studying the masters in Europe, doggedly attempting to copy, to conform, to fit in with accepted artistic norms of her time. But then something happened. After years of frustrations, setbacks, and artistic dry spells, she finally let go of all preconceived notions and accepted ideas about art when it came to painting on canvas. She found her own glorious form of expression. Nature, with a capital 'N', was at the core of her artistry. Once she let her spirit speak, the forest trees she put to canvas came alive. One day, she snatched up her pencil and excitedly sketched an indigenous face mask peering out from intertwining tree branches. She had made the connection between a spiritual life force and material representation; she was on her way. The tree paintings of her final years are magnificent, the full expression of what she had wanted to say all along.

A dragonfly the size of a bird. A frog the size of my thumbnail. The hoot of an owl as I drift off to sleep. Something about all of it pulls on my heart, as if I won't have all of this on my doorstep forever. There's a sense that our time in Topsfield is waning, though we don't know what is in store. We must dislodge our roots from this time and place in order to arrive at the next. It's not the first time I have had to prepare for this, and it won't be the last. Life is always about hanging between two points. Being is always becoming. It's so easy to forget this. One minute a dragonfly is oozy, larval, floating on the scrim of pond water, no more capable of flying than a pebble. The next, it's fluttering its tiny mesh wings above our back deck in the sun as bed sheets flap on the laundry line and a songbird eyes it for lunch.

Though I built my shed on the edge of the ravine to be separate, a place apart, I make note that my shed is sitting atop the surface of molten rock on a planet spinning in space. It is as much subject to the laws of gravity, decay, and regeneration as I am. As the visits from my former selves have confirmed, there is no separateness to be had. For better or worse, everything is in relationship with everything else: A root with a rock, a spider with a dragonfly, a shed with a ravine, a breeze with a bird, a body with a soul, the seen with the unseen, the present with the past. Everywhere and everything across time and space is in unending and rapturous relationship.

I take myself to the back porch to watch the dying of the day. The glow from a triple-wicked candle gains prominence as shadows begin to deepen. Songbirds and peepers are calling and crying out across the ravine. My shed gradually dissolves into darkness creeping through the woodlands, so that only the white outline of its door remains visible—almost ghostly—across the back clearing. With the ceiling light illuminating me from above, the glow of the candle in front of me, and darkness enfolding the porch, my full self is reflected in the sliding glass doors. As I blow out the candle flame, a question arises from the tendrils of smoke, and I hear the voices of all the selves that were ever me joining in the refrain of my one miraculous and resurrected life: *If lumps of clay and tree ash can transform into something else of beauty and purpose, then what about you?*

Works Cited

Preface – Portents of a New Life

Andrews, Ted. Animal-Speak: *The Spiritual and Magical Powers of Creatures Great and Small*. St, Paul. MN: Llewelyn Publications 1988, p. 280.

Campbell, Joseph, ed. Betty Sue Flowers. *The Power of Myth with Bill Moyers*. New York: Doubleday (Anchor Books) 1988, p. 115.

Chapter 1 – The Green of All Green

Associated Press. "These Rocks Make Strange Journeys." USA Today, Aug. 29, 2014, p. 9A.

Rawlings, Marjorie Kinnan. *Cross Creek*. New York: TOUCHSTONE (Simon & Schuster Inc.) 1996, p. 45.

Chapter 3 – So Full of Gladness

De Mello, Anthony, S.J. *The Way to Love*. New York: Doubleday 1992 (Image Books Edition 1995), p.85.

Stedman, Edmund Clarence. *Poets of America; Ralph Waldo Emerson*. Boston and New York: Houghton Mifflin and Company, The Riverside Press 1885, p. 173.

Gardner, Kevin. *The Granite Kiss: Traditions and Techniques of Building New England Stone Walls*. Woodstock, VT: The Countryman Press 2001, p. 170.

Oliver, Mary. *Thirst: Poems by Mary Oliver*. Boston: Beacon Press 2006, p.4.

Whiteley, Opal Stanley. *The Fairyland Around Us*. Los Angeles: Publisher's Printing Co. 1918.

Chapter 4 – Boundaries Are Porous

Volf, Miroslav. *The End of Memory: Remembering Rightly in a Violent World.* Grand Rapids, MI/Cambridge UK: Wm. B. Eerdmans Publishing Co. 2006, p. 73.

Chapter 5 – The Listening Post

Harter, Michael, S.J. *Hearts on Fire: Praying with the Jesuits.* St. Louis, MO: The Institute of Jesuit Sources 1993, p. 10.

Thoreau, Henry David. *Walking.* Bedford, MA: Applewood Books 1992. ("Walking" was originally published in *The Atlantic Monthly*, June 1862).

Chapter 6 – All the Questions and Answers of the Universe

Shadbolt, Doris. *Seven Journeys: The Sketchbooks of Emily Carr.* Vancouver, British Columbia: Douglas & McIntyre 2002, p. 62.

Chapter 9 – Heaven Is an Unmown Field

L'Engle, Madeleine. *A Ring of Endless Light.* New York: Farrar Straus Giroux 1980.

Longfellow, Henry Wadsworth, ed. J.D. McClatchy. *Poems and Other Writings.* New York: Literary Classics of the United States, Inc. 2000, p. 627.

Chapter 10 – Life Is Short

Lamott, Anne. *Help Thanks Wow: The Three Essential Prayers.* Detroit: Thorndike Press 2012.

Okakura, Kakuzo. *The Book of Tea.* Tokyo/New York/London: Kodansha International 2005.

Rupp, Joyce. *Walk in a Relaxed Manner: Life Lessons from the Camino.* MaryKnoll, NY: Orbis Books 2005.

Kurutz, Steven. "Q&A: A Religious Retreat All His Own." The New York Times, Oct. 16, 2014.

Chapter 11 – Death Without Dying

Lane, Margaret. *The Tale of Beatrix Potter: A Biography*. London and New York: Frederick Warne & Co., Inc. 1946, p. 85.

Chapter 12 – "Ravine Syndrome" or the Sacred Swamp

Cameron, Julia. *The Artist's Way: A Spiritual Path to Higher Creativity*. New York: Jeremy P. Tarcher/Putnam of Penguin Putman, Inc. 2002, p. 18.

Kaufman, Kenn & Kimberly. *Kaufman Field Guide to the Nature of New England*. New York: Houghton Mifflin Harcourt 2012.

Thoreau, Henry David, ed. Brooks Atkinson. *Walden and Other Writings*. New York: Random House, Inc. (The Modern Library) 1992, p.92.

Melville, Herman. *Moby-Dick*. New York: Alfred A. Knopf, Inc. (Everyman's Library) 1907.

Walker, Alice. *The Color Purple*. New York: Washington Square Press POCKET BOOKS (Simon & Schuster, Inc.) 1982.

Welty, Eudora. *The Optimist's Daughter*. New York: Random House 1969.

About the Author

Barbara R. Bodengraven, M.T.S., Weston Jesuit School of Theology, is a writer and communications professional dedicated to advancing matters of spirituality and religious faith as compelling and crucial issues for our time.

She has written for the Harvard Divinity School quarterly journal, the *Bulletin*, and served as a communications professional and consultant for the Sisters of Notre Dame de Namur, Episcopal Divinity School, Trinity Church Boston, and Weston Jesuit School of Theology, where she served as the editor of its quarterly magazine, *Light & Life*.

With a certificate in Youth & Young Adult Ministry from the Boston Theological Institute, B.R. Bodengraven conducts spiritual writing workshops for youth as well as adults, helping people explore and develop their intuitive—yet often overlooked and under-appreciated—spiritual insights and identity.

For more information about 'The Sacred Shed' Writing Workshops, contact B.R. Bodengraven at: thesacredshed@gmail.com.

Made in the USA
Middletown, DE
14 January 2018